Negotiating Empowerment

Studies in English Language Education

Premakumari Dheram

Orient Longman

ORIENT LONGMAN PRIVATE LIMITED

Registered Office
3-6-752 Himayatnagar, Hyderabad 500 029 (A.P.), India
Email: cogeneral@orientlongman.com

Other Offices
Bangalore / Bhopal / Bhubaneshwar / Chennai
Ernakulam / Guwahati / Hyderabad / Jaipur / Kolkata
Lucknow / Mumbai / New Delhi / Patna

First published 2008

ISBN 13: 978 81 250 3231 1
ISBN 10: 81 250 3231 2

Typeset in Aldine401 BT 10.5/12.6pt
OSDATA, Hyderabad 500 029

Printed in India at
Graphica Printers
Hyderabad 500 013

Published by
Orient Longman Private Limited
3-6-752 Himayatnagar
Hyderabad 500 029 (A.P.), India
Email: hydgeneral@orientlongman.com

Dedication

To my late teacher Professor Isaac Sequeira,
who taught me that living is a means of reaching out

Contents

Foreword

A majority of the contributions to this anthology, that brings together voices and viewpoints from countries across several continents, deal with English language at work in contexts of life and learning. They differ on how they view its presence as also on what or where to look for helpful ways to respond to the real or perceived needs of individuals or of their societies.

A couple of related issues come to mind in viewing the English language as part of the early 21st century language education in India. Both should have relevance to other countries where too English language shares classroom space with one or more indigenous languages. A brief word on each will constitute this foreword. My hope is that it will relate to parts of what this rich resource on language use for human empowerment offers.

One, for the first time ever, English language for every child who enters a primary school is becoming part of State-level educational policy in both urban and rural India. With over six hundred and sixty thousand primary schools at work, the challenges that arise in translating that decision into effective schoolroom practice are immense, but the opportunities are far greater. Questioned on grounds, both linguistic and educational, this bold decision is essentially a legislative response to the legitimate aspirations of millions across India who, despite the constitutional guarantee of equity of access, have experienced educational deprival for over five decades. However, significant questions on its practicality remain at least partially unanswered. What are the options?

Sceptics who merely highlight existing failures caused by inadequate human resources or the inability to utilise the means that exist achieve little. They do, however, remind the profession of the need to press into service old and emerging means capable of making a fuller exposure to the language possible for every child in school. English language as the medium to teach a core school subject is, for example, receiving serious attention in some states; so is a fuller use of technologies, not excluding those with support in educational satellites. The true option is to move forward with a studied understanding of the realities on the ground and the optimum use of appropriate and affordable resources, human and material.

Two, powerful expressions of the need to redesign language curricula in full awareness of the country's multilingual-multicultural environment (e.g. National Curriculum Framework: NCERT 2005—) have come at the right time. For far too long the ELT system has remained suspicious of the place of the learner's language in the English classroom. A main reason has been the forcefully promoted belief that the monolingual alternatives imported in several different forms over a half century (1950s—) replaced the non-functional grammar translation method (GTM) that relied on ill-informed grammar and unregulated translation. With support in the native-English speaking world, it claims that the imported alternatives have brought in a succession of informed methodologies, each measurably better than all that existed before as also what it partially or fully managed to replace. The methodological progression is thus presented not as several swings of the pendulum wherein each one, in adding something new, displaces something of proven value but as 'a path of upward progress from method to better method' (Pennycook 2000: 275).

Two questions demand answers in confronting this dominant belief: 'Did the 'alternative methods' replace nothing but the non-functional GTM'?' and 'Were the views on Indian languages in English classrooms the same as those that have prevailed since the import of the alternatives?'. Brief references to what existed during the early years of the 20th century long before the system embraced the alternatives should, besides providing the answers, help set the record right. They may also help the planner smooth the path to a more appropriate alternative.

A look back

a. The ideational base

Viewing ELT inside a bilingual education system was part of contemporary wisdom almost a full century ago. So was the awareness that India's own languages needed far greater acceptance and attention. Known too was the belief, with support in data-driven research and practice, that working in harmony two or more languages inside a language classroom became mutually supportive and markedly more productive. The much maligned GTM did not add up to all that was known or sponsored in India, even eighty or more years ago; nor was it the preferred option. A few relevant facts with brief excerpts in their support should serve to foreground parts of what existed. The fuller answers can only come from a documented history of Indian ELT, which as of now does not exist.

In convening an education conference in 1901, Lord Curzon had made it known that contrary to what many of his influential countrymen (including Lord Macaulay of the 1835 *Minute* fame) had made the policy makers believe, Indian languages had all the potential to take the place of English in school education: 'We started by too slavish imitation of English models, and to this day, we have never purged ourselves of the taint . . . If the vernaculars contained no literary models, no classics, I might not be willing to recommend them. But we all know that in them are enshrined famous treasures of literature.' A year later, in 1902, the Indian Universities Commission reiterated that understanding to assert that 'Unless . . . a good training in the vernacular is given in the schools, no effort of the University will avail.'

Fifteen years on, in 1917, a high-level Commission to study Calcutta University was at work. The Commission's octavo-size 13-volume report (1919) stands out for many insights into not just Calcutta University or university education in general but, in good measure, into education as a whole. One of the subjects it focused its attention on was languages in education. Here is part of what it said.

Highlighting the fact that the learner's mother tongue 'as an instrument of mental training' had for long been neglected in the school system partly because of the introduction of English as the chief medium, it pointed out that 'The premature use of a foreign, and half understood, medium in teaching the ordinary subjects of the school curriculum tends to produce intellectual muddle, which is concealed more or less at the matriculation test by remarkable feats of memorization, but made plain where the new stage of the university is reached' (Vol 5: 29–30).

Asserting that there was something gravely wrong with a system of education which, at the end of school, left young persons incapable of expressing themselves in writing as in speaking in their mother tongue, it made a strong case for the use of the learner's first language as the medium at the secondary school for all subjects other than English and mathematics and, importantly, emphasised the need to make 'English and the Indian vernacular languages co-ordinate factors in working out . . . a harmonious combination of Eastern and Western civilization' (ibid: 50). Also, to provide meaningful assistance to the early stages of education, it emphatically expressed the desirability of making systematic efforts to promote the serious study of vernaculars at all levels in the educational system (ibid: 58–60). There followed specific recommendations for language education in schools, colleges and universities. Two of those were that the vernacular should be used in general throughout the high school except for the teaching of English and mathematics—which during the four years of the course, should be conducted in English—and that in the university, a distinction should be made between the teaching of English for practical and for literary purposes; teaching of both kinds should be available to all students, but a uniform course in English literature should not be a compulsory subject for all students in the arts faculty.

b. From theory to practice

As for the adoption of that policy in schools and the approaches to its why and how, one needs to look at books on the subject that followed soon after. Four years on in 1923, a first such book, *Teaching of English*, by Wyatt carried forward the belief into language classrooms. Wyatt aimed at an all-skills proficiency in English. To make those aims effective, he singled out the need to pay attention to both the learner's L1 and English in the belief that a main reason for failures in English teaching was the system's neglect of the mother tongue which was taught by poorly paid and unskilled teachers. He went further to assert that the teacher of English was expected to make the best use of the pupil's knowledge of his mother tongue.

Wyatt next related that thesis to another. On 'How to speak well, read well, and enjoy good reading', he asserted, 'there are methods of teaching each of these to the pupil whatever language he speaks, or writes, or reads' and importantly, that the 'language habits thus acquired hold good whatever language be his medium'(ibid: 107). Having then reiterated his belief by adding that 'the right habits taught in one language will overflow into the pupil's use of any other language', he supplemented it with focused advice to the practitioner-reader. 'What I wish to impress upon my reader', he wrote, 'is the importance of establishing an understanding between the teacher of the vernacular and the teacher of English as to the part that each is to play in the teaching of these arts and a conscious and systematic cooperation between them' (ibid: 107). The book provided illustrated examples to show how that aim could be realised by teachers in teaching different aspects/elements of the language.

Three years on in *Bilingualism* (1926), a book that brought together the results of many years of classroom-based experiments, Michael West provided data-driven support to his thesis that reading ability transferred fully across languages (on this, see also Tickoo 1988, 1990, 1991). Having next found out in a number of experimental classrooms that 'the practice-effect in English reading is transferred to Bengali reading' and having studied the gains thus made over a period of time, he concluded that 'Reading ability is a *general power*. It is not confined to one language: for improvement in the ability to read one language is transferred and shows itself in improvement of the reading of another language' (West 1926).

That reading is a general power which transfers from language to language received little attention inside India then or thereafter. However, some sixty years on, it began to find support in longitudinal research and study (e.g. the Canadian immersion programme: see Cummins and Swain 1986, Cummins and Nakajima 1987, Harley et al 1990). It continues to receive support in applied linguistics scholarship.

Summing Up

What I have pointed out with modest support in relevant literature of the early 20th century can be put in three brief statements: One, that the need to make use of the learner's mother tongue was part of the system that preceded the reformist agenda and the imported wisdom of the last half century by several decades. Two, that the desirability of making the learner's own language and English partners in effective language education existed and had found expression in books on ELT. Three, that the methods in use in that period were not at all confined to the GTM. They included those that focused on all skills and also others that saw wisdom in making reading the main means to language proficiency. A possible inference is that the recent expressions of the need for English language to be placed in multilingual contexts and made to work in harmony with Indian languages had their antecedents in what got written and, in some measure, practised almost a century ago.

Makhan Lal Tickoo
November 2007

Acknowledgements

This book has been possible because of many people, scholars, students and institutions, and their commitment to learning. Without their help and encouragement, I would not have had this opportunity to contribute to the dialogue on the politics of English language education. I am thankful to the following persons and institutions.

My father, Sridhara Dheram, introduced me to the philosophical foundations of education years ago. I returned to his book on the subject when I could no longer postpone answering questions regarding my own role as a second language teacher.

At about the same time, in 2000, George Braine asked me to reflect on my growth as an English teacher; and, I began to read and think about myself and a host of other things.

Soon, I learned that everyone has strong opinions about the relationship between individual, society and education. My mother, Anuradha, for example, has her own views on education, having taught her children and grandchildren and having seen them through university education.

For an in-depth understanding, however, I needed help from educational philosophers and English teachers who thought critically about their own role in education. I am fortunate I live in a city where there are universities and great libraries—EFL University (formerly, the Central Institute of English and Foreign Languages), Osmania University and Osmania University Centre for International Programmes (formerly, ASRC and IACIS)—and also that their staff are most dependable.

In May 2004, my reading acquired a wider meaning and purpose when Professor Isaac Sequeira (then Director, IACIS) encouraged me to organise an international seminar on effective (English) language management in SAARC countries.

The project acquired a professional tone thanks to Professor M.L. Tickoo and Professor Champa Tickoo.

Friends Nitya Rani, Srinivas, Appa Swami and Subramanyam Raju gave tremendous physical and emotional support throughout the project.

Several scholars including Alan Maley, Alastair Pennycook, Christopher Brumfit and Robert Phillipson sent their best wishes.

The contributors believed in my ability to edit the seminar proceedings.

Professor John McRae gave helpful suggestions on my paper.

The work gathered momentum when Orient Longman responded positively to my request for publishing the book and shouldered the responsibility of taking the project forward.

Kiran, Suma and Indu have been great as friends, counsellors, critics and secretaries.

Thank you so much, everyone. I will always be indebted to you.

Editor

Overview

Negotiating Empowerment: Studies in English Language Education is a contributory volume of papers that examines the relationship between English language pedagogy and identity. The authors, from different parts of the world, including India, Hong Kong, Pakistan, Sri Lanka, Switzerland and the USA, share two main concerns. First, language education cannot continue to be a weapon of cultural, economic, emotional and social control. In a world which is more bilingual or multilingual than monolingual, it is natural for people to use different languages for different purposes. This natural linguistic diversity has to be respected, and also needs to be accommodated in the curriculum. Second, critical enquiry into the nature of language use, learning and teaching in bilingual and multilingual contexts will help depoliticise and reconceptualise language education. This is both a concern and a challenge that the language teacher and the learner must negotiate within the classroom, with the support of the state.

Section I: Towards critical English language learning and teaching

Premakumari Dheram's paper 'Empowerment through Enquiry' highlights the need for reconceptualising English language education, with special focus on critical enquiry. Given the nature of language as an instrument of power, the author argues that in multilingual countries such as India, language pedagogy must have two interrelated aims. It must raise the stakeholders' awareness of the political nature of their position and initiate the process of their negotiating it to empower themselves. This will help them acquire useful insights into their role as policy makers, parents, teachers, learners, material writers and examiners. Dheram suggests that universities should launch initiatives in this direction. As the first step, they may evolve a curriculum that encourages the teacher and learner to examine pedagogic practices in a wide sociopolitical context. Further, the state should identify research into language pedagogy as an urgent concern and support it.

Rama Kant Agnihotri in 'Language, Literacy Practices and English' examines the parameters of language development in developing societies, paying special attention to how multilingualism, especially in the case of Asia, includes various oral traditions and literacy practices. Every domain in the Asian countries, however, reflects the power of English and reveals how the language controls different resources. Agnihotri shows that language management in such contexts must address the future of SAARC languages and not that of English, and that the focus should be on how 'English can . . . reach out to the marginalised sections of the society and empower them', and how we can make sure that their languages are not 'damaged in the process'. The author believes that such issues must be examined, and he identifies the classroom as the site where it must be done. He also suggests that collaboration between various governmental and non-governmental agencies supported by technology may help 'elevate the status of other languages and literacy practices'.

In 'Language Planning Scholarship: Towards Adequacy', Thiru Kandiah argues that planning for English and its teaching and learning in postcolonial settings, especially in SAARC countries, leaves the most important explanatory questions unrecognised. What it does at most is to legitimise the hegemonic status quo in the sociopolitical arena 'out there' (both local and global). Kandiah argues that an effort to engage with the problematic necessarily puts the whole scholarly discipline of language planning on trial, challenging it particularly along its metatheoretical dimensions. With the focus on the situation in Sri Lanka, he explores how the discipline may be released from the stultifying limits which it currently suffers from, by virtue of its entrapment within perspectives determined by the metropolitan centres, to enable the complexities of the very different postcolonial contexts. This will both extend and enhance language planning metatheory, and also enable the discipline to turn itself to useful account for the very large numbers of ordinary human subjects who, though habitually sidelined by a privileged scholarship and research, ultimately lie at the heart of all these exertions, whether scholarly or otherwise.

In 'Patterns of Bilingualism in the New World Order: The South Asian Scene', K. Chellappan describes the role of various languages in forging identity and unity in terms of culture. According to him, 'this unity is more a recovery than a discovery'. While English has emerged as a global language, other languages have also made their legitimate claims in the new world order. Bilingualism, or even multilingualism, has become the order of the day and has contributed to the dialogic interaction between and within nations. If English has become the medium of communication and source of information the world over, regional languages such as Swahili (East Africa), Hausa (West Africa), Chinese, Hindi and many other languages are becoming increasingly important at the national and regional levels. Chellappan says that a policy of interpenetration of languages for mutual benefit must inform the pedagogy and percolate the classroom. Such a convergence is possible even between regional languages, and English can play a mediating role in this.

In 'English and Globalisation: Language Management in Cross-Cultural Settings', L. M. Khubchandani discusses, primarily, two issues of language management, with the focus on how different languages project reality through different conceptual systems. He provides a brief overview of the postcolonial situation in India, where the non-native speaker has to use English for crosscultural purposes, and has also to learn to deal with problems of indeterminacy. Translation, in such situations, becomes an important mechanism of communication. Khubchandani describes a few problems of translating from Sanskrit into English, and suggests that the translator take note of the differences in conceptual systems while translating from one language into another. The second issue that the author focuses on is how the use of English, associated with status and power, contributes to an atmosphere of distrust, between the English-speaking elite and the masses. Given the situation, Khubchandani says that both the educated Indian and the state have a responsible role to play in developing Indian languages and in depoliticising the process.

Probal Dasgupta in 'Sustainable Scenarios in Indian Language Cultivation' identifies the 'presence of English with the industrial hijack of the cognitive' in countries like India. He argues that 'the intellectual centre of gravity has been permitted to shift to English, with very similar consequences' whether English is a second or a foreign language. In this context, he examines two models with regard to the anglophone–Indian identity construction. One involves the formation of a 'strong boundary' between the haves and the have-nots, and the rejection of Indian languages for defining modernity. It also excludes the rural base of the Indian identity completely. Most sadly, it involves the consumption of knowledge produced in the West. The alternative model, which Dasgupta recommends, projects India as a 'knowledge-producing site' and all Indians as partners facilitating the production of a 'host narrative qua arena' instead of a 'master narrative qua foundation'. It is in this direction that the media and pedagogy must make a concerted effort.

Stefano Vassere, in 'The Role of English and Language Teaching in Switzerland' situation presents the volatile linguistic situation in the country in the context of English emerging as the lingua franca within the Swiss community. There are three national languages in Switzerland—French, German and Italian. The people in different regions have different attitudes towards language teaching, and school policies are formulated locally. More importantly, the increasing use of English at the workplace has given rise to the fear that Switzerland 'will remain isolated from the international community' without the advantage of English. Such 'economic factors' are cited in support of reforms which include not only the introduction of English early at school but also the replacement of one of the national languages at school with English. Further, as Vassere argues, the Italian region which believes in teaching two national languages together with English 'is the most penalised'.

In 'A Second Look at English as a Window on the World That Has Changed', Jacob Tharu examines the goals that have guided English teaching in India since Independence. Although English has been identified as the library language, acquisition of skills, either productive or receptive, has received very little attention in our education. Not surprisingly, there is no awareness of the importance of receptive skills in accessing knowledge related to modernisation. Qualifying in various competitive examinations rather than acquiring a reasonable command of English has been the big concern relating to the teaching and learning of the language. What is required is a changed perspective towards listening and reading as active processes that are supported by a wide range of content and that sharpen critical skills. The student citizen must realise that he/she needs 'a sound base of overall proficiency' in English to be proactive in engaging with the 'richer world' that exists beyond the 'brainwashing' and 'intrusive pop-ups' on the Internet.

E. Annamalai's paper, 'Equalising Access to English in Education and Balancing Multilingualism in India', discusses two fallacies related to the teaching and learning of English. The author points out that both parents and the state seem to think that the teaching of English must begin from class 1. However, the huge numbers, inadequate human resources and pedagogic inefficiency make the early introduction of English at the school impracticable. The second fallacy is that all subjects must be taught through the medium of English. In the Indian context, Annamalai recommends that we evolve methods for teaching the language skills first in L1, and then transferring them to L2. The principles of pedagogy support this approach as it will help develop the cognitive potential of all the learners, including the first generation learner, whose home environment does not reinforce English. Annamalai points out that successful teaching of English means successful teaching of the student's mother tongue.

In 'Mother Language Education and Cognitive Development', V. Prakasam shows how the term mother language defies precision. He says that any attempt to make it focused will make it inapplicable to real situations; and an attempt to broad-base it will make its link with cognitive development weak. Cognitive development, subsumed under maturation, comprises cognition, conceptualisation and relationalisation, which are not single processes. In this context, Prakasam examines the role played by mother language education in multilingual societies.

Robert Bellarmine's paper, 'Mother Tongue and the Other Tongues: A Plea for Balance and Action', identifies the beliefs in relation to language use in SAARC countries, and argues for a formula for estimating the value of activities in our mother tongues. The fact that English is elbowing out our languages makes their promotion an immediate sociopolitical concern.

Citing the findings of a case study he conducted, Bellarmine highlights the need for improving the teaching of the mother tongue in order to save it. He recommends an integrated approach to language teaching which focuses on the universal nature of the four skills and the possibility of skill transfer across languages. The SAARC countries may collaborate with the British Council in this regard, and benefit from their expertise in the areas of 'teaching, research, materials production, testing, and management of learning concerned with English'. The British, on the other hand, would have an opportunity to appreciate the richness of other languages and literatures. Bellarmine also suggests that formulas may be evolved for assessing the economic benefits of language activities in education, business, and overseas aid. In his view, this is essential for sensitising the stakeholders in the modern tendency to 'evaluate things predominantly in economic terms'.

Section II: Critical classroom practices

In 'Postmodern Epistemology and Causality: Research Theory and Application at the Crossroads', aimed at educational evaluators and classroom teachers, Dale T. Griffee argues that we are in the midst of a change in the underlying theory of educational evaluation, from one termed as the standard view to one not yet agreed on. He further argues that the change in philosophical orientation is important because of implications for classroom evaluation and teaching. Griffee presents a three-part model contrasting positivism and post-positivism in terms of theory (specific philosophical context, approach, causality model) and application (research design, data collection and analysis), and shows that post-positivism using a realist model of causality is best suited for contemporary educational evaluation because (a) it seeks to identify causality within the context of the study, and (b) it allows for the use of quantitative and qualitative data analysis.

George Stanley Braine's paper, 'Implementing Writing Across the Curriculum (WAC) in Hong Kong', describes an innovative WAC programme that was implemented at three universities in Hong Kong. While based on the models offered at American universities, the programme in Hong Kong (probably the first to be implemented in Asia) was adapted to suit the needs of teachers and students who are mainly non-native speakers of English functioning in an English as a Foreign Language (EFL) context. Braine notes that in the past two years, the programme has benefited a large number of students enrolled in more than fifty courses across disciplines, and has created a community of interdisciplinary scholars committed to the improvement of teaching and learning. WAC is especially relevant for English language enhancement because tight degree plans leave most students with little opportunity to take writing courses offered by English departments and centres. Indeed, by incorporating writing in English into courses in their majors, students will enhance their English proficiency while improving their thinking skills.

The majority of the world's population functions in more than one language for social, professional and educational purposes. In this context, Greta J. Gorsuch's 'Adults Becoming Bilingual and Becoming Teachers: Pushing Outside the Comfort Zone' is a case study of adults who become functionally bilingual through becoming teachers in their second language. Gorsuch describes three groups, Japanese high school English teachers, international teaching assistants from 'external L2' countries, and international teaching assistants from 'indigenised practice L2' settings. The circumstances surrounding each group are characterised, and the language choices these bilinguals make in response to these circumstances and to individual needs are contrasted with the consequences these choices imply. 'Language choices' here means an adult bilingual choosing to interact with other speakers of the L2, to limit their interaction to teacher/student settings or to expand their interaction for social purposes. The study highlights the intersections between social identity, language choices and language learning theory.

In 'Higher Education and Gender in Pakistan: Issues and Concerns for Language Planning,' Sabiha Mansoor discusses how women's access to higher education is limited, and how it affects their socioeconomic status and employment opportunities. In this context, her study focuses on the concerns about the limited role of regional languages, lack of required materials in Urdu, and student difficulties in English. Mansoor says that the low self-esteem of Pakistani female students may be attributed to their low social and economic status in society, and this in turn is related to their unequal participation in higher education. The problem is compounded by the low ethnolinguistic vitality of regional speakers, especially the speakers of the Punjabi language. Mansoor's study highlights the need for a state policy on education to protect women's rights to higher education and promote positive attitudes towards minority languages in Pakistan. This will arrest the process of language shift among the ethnic minority female students in the country.

In 'Merging of Context and Methodology: MEd in TESOL Curriculum in Sri Lanka', Marie Perera examines the relevance of western-based TESOL programmes for non-native English speakers (NNSs) who intend to teach in their home countries. Many of these programmes do not address the issues specific to the non-native context and, hence, the relevance of such training becomes an important issue with regard to the ESL curriculum. Perera says that the reasons for very little success in the teaching of English in Sri Lanka, could be in part due to the use of a predominantly methodological approach in training teachers, which makes no attempt to equip them with the tools to understand the context in which learning and teaching take place. The paper describes an initiative that tries to bridge the gap between 'metropolitan' and 'peripheral' contexts and to merge methodology and context. The proposed Master of Education programme in Teaching of English to Speakers of Other Languages (MEd in TESOL) at the Faculty of Education, University of Colombo, is an attempt to contextualise ELT within a Sri Lankan as well as an Asian context.

Arifa Rahman's paper, 'Towards a Culturally-Friendly Approach to ESL Teacher Development in Bangladesh', argues that the greater the importance attached to education as a whole, the higher is the priority that needs to be accorded to the teachers responsible for that education. She describes the series of steps Bangladesh has taken towards curricular reform since the late 1980s with focus on the importance of teachers' construction of knowledge, their interpretation of the world around them, and their orientation towards teaching. Highlighting the ongoing and cooperative nature of teacher development, the author shows that such reform has to be sustained through a supportive infrastructure over a long period. The experiments, Rahman says, recommend a long-term investment in a total system rather than a one-off arrangement.

Section I

Towards Critical English Language Learning and Teaching

1

Empowerment through Enquiry

Premakumari Dheram

In any multilingual country, it is imperative that the curriculum provide for a critical dialogue on the politics of language. As users and educators, we must address questions of our linguistic and cultural identity, especially in the context of the spread of English. Contrary to popular and academic conceptions, English has never been just a 'link' or 'library' language, and the epithets 'non-native speaker/teacher/learner' and 'second language teacher/learner' echo a sense of marginality and displacement (Braine 2005, Cummins 1996, Kachru 1982, Rampton 1990 and Shondel 2005). This is because '. . . language itself is content, a referent for loyalties and animosities, an indicator of social statuses and personal relationships, a marker of situations and topics as well as of the societal goals and the large-scale value-laden arenas of interaction . . .' (Fishman 1972, 4). It is in this context that the need to understand the nature of empowerment in relation to English and evolve formal educational interventions for negotiating it becomes a serious and urgent concern.

As the history of the world shows, policies of education influence the course of the development of different languages (Braine 2005, Pennycook 1994, Skutnabb-Kangas and Phillipson 1994, Tollefson 2002). The promotion of English in India, for example, has led to numerous problems which have been the subject of an ongoing debate in both academic and non-academic forums (Agnihotri and Khanna 1997, Annamalai 1992, Khubchandani 1991). Despite the monumental efforts of the state and private agencies, the percentage of the population that can make full use of the opportunities to learn English and enjoy the accompanying economic and social privileges continues to be small. It cannot be denied that the gap between the English haves and the English have-nots is only getting wider. The social and official endorsement of the promotion of English, and the inability of academic institutions to provide first generation and rural learners with the support structure essential for learning the language have bred a great deal of insecurity accompanied by low self-esteem. Indeed, it is not easy 'to break the vicious association between English and social status in India' (Ram 1991, 52). Further, most of our young English medium-educated learners of today have a different inadequacy to live with. They cannot read or write in their first language, and share this 'handicap' with well-known Indian writers like Tharoor (2005, 5–6), who says, 'What about Indian books? Sadly, I suffered a major handicap: my parents' peripatetic life. . . cut me off from the literature of my mother tongue, Malayalam. As with other children of migratory Indians, English became not only the language of my schoolbooks but of my private life: I played with my friends in English, quarrelled with my sisters in English, wrote to my relatives in English—and read for pleasure in English. The colonial inheritance made this a common predicament among urban, English-educated Indians.' Thus, economic and intellectual empowerment, as the goal of English language education, has come to mean emotional and cultural disempowerment too. This appears to be the case with English learners in many countries (Canagarajah 2004, Ibrahim 1999, Pennycook 1994).

Higher education in English: limitations

As Tickoo (1994, 332) says, 'English in India continues to be taught as though it were a language of social survival rather than a strong additional language whose unique contributions lie in relating scientific and technological developments to the country's socioeconomic needs, aspirations and challenges'. The conceptual thinness in our second language educational context must be attributed to the fact that English teachers and learners do not view themselves as instruments of self-affirmation. This is because they do not have the opportunity to realise the value of critical enquiry into the use and pedagogy of the English language which will equip them with the intellectual tools to negotiate the tensions of second language education in a multilingual context. Beliefs and values can form the basis of pedagogy only with adequate theoretical support. However, unfortunately, very little graduate and postgraduate research is encouraged in this direction. This is the reason why higher education in English has contributed very few insights to the teaching and learning of the language. The seriousness of such implications, especially in a multilingual country, is yet to be recognised by universities.

The absence of a strong tradition of critical enquiry into English language education has prevented us from realising that pedagogy is a tool of intellection and independence. This has also been responsible for the lack of critical consciousness regarding the relationship between language and development. The fact that teaching is an interactive process between society and the classroom is often ignored and questions of culture, development, equal opportunities, identity, and most importantly self-esteem do not form a part of the English language curriculum. Very few university departments of English recognise the importance of examining pedagogy or formal educational interventions in relation to a specific educational context despite their awareness of the key role languages play in the empowerment, and disempowerment, of the individual and the state. Fewer departments develop advanced research libraries in this area. In other words, there is no mechanism which can guide the teacher or the student of English away from the linguistically and culturally oppressive social conditions created by the media and the economy. In sum, the teaching community has failed to evolve indigenous critical tools without which empowerment remains only a dream.

Given the situation, what opportunities do learners have to appreciate that English language education means more than an economic opportunity? And, what guidance do first generation learners have to understand that higher education in/through English is an opportunity to locate themselves more emotionally than economically? Such educational, context-specific issues demand immediate attention. How does one identify the issues? Why and how should they be explored? How do pedagogical practices determine the way the various components of an educational context are located politically? What kind of practices help the teacher and the learner understand their political positions in the context of language use and language learning? What practices help them counter the negative forces which limit their potential for growth into effective language users? Most importantly, how is an individual's growth as a language user related to the cultural development of his society? Is the former possible without the latter?

The teacher

It seems to me that the 'how' of teaching and learning has always been on the back burner where our English language education is concerned, and that this has pushed the teacher, as Freire (1970, 46) observes, into the position of a 'narrating subject' who 'makes deposits which the students patiently receive, memorize, and repeat. . . In the banking concept of education . . . the teacher presents himself to his students as their necessary opposite'. This perception of the role of a teacher is further reinforced by training and refresher programmes which seem to focus only on narration. Equally important are the teacher-evaluation questionnaires which include questions on the teachers' awareness of the subject, their preparation, punctuality and regularity and the fairness of assessment of students. The teacher's awareness of critical enquiry, which is central to education, does not find any mention at all. Thus, the content of training programmes and evaluation questionnaires subscribes to and promotes the banking concept of education and a reductive role of the teacher in higher education. Unfortunately, the self-perception of the teacher, in most cases, is conditioned by this image and very few English teachers consider themselves students of either the language or pedagogy.

This has done the greatest damage in the context of the teaching of English as a second language. English teachers, instead of examining the processes of teaching and learning the language in the specific educational context and evolving their own pedagogy, accept the methods and materials imported from the West. They thus, accept the supremacy of not only the language but also the pedagogical practices. Although disappointed with the consignment, which is more often than not ineffective in their multilingual, heterogeneous and large classes, they fail to evolve any indigenous practices for lack of orientation and infrastructure. Thus, the English teacher becomes an agent of cultural invasion in more than one sense.

The learner

The undue emphasis on the teacher as a giver has not only encouraged teacher dependence but has also prevented the learner from evaluating the value of the 'deposits' made by the teacher. Very few students realise that 'in the banking system of education' they 'have the opportunity to become collectors or cataloguers of the things they store. But, in the last analysis, it is men themselves who are filed away through the lack of creativity, transformation, and knowledge in this (at best) misguided system. For apart from inquiry, apart from praxis, men cannot be truly human. Knowledge emerges only through invention and re-invention, through the restless, impatient, continuing, hopeful inquiry men pursue in the world, with the world, and with each other' (Freire 1970, 46). Unfortunately, few academic programmes in English consider learner autonomy to be the goal of higher education; and rarely does the curriculum create a forum for critical enquiry into the personal and social relevance of English language education.

The process of understanding that every language and, hence, every language speaker is equal does not happen automatically. Indeed, 'the more students work at storing the deposits entrusted to them, the less they develop the critical consciousness which would result from their intervention in the world as transformers of that world. The more completely they accept the passive role imposed on them, the more they tend simply to adapt to the world as it is and to the fragmented view of reality deposited in them' (ibid, 47). What students (and teachers) of English and other major languages require is a critical awareness to appreciate the need for understanding their role in changing the existing social structure to create equal opportunities to speakers of all languages. They must be sensitive to the relationship between curriculum and identity construction. Without a curriculum which addresses the role of language and development in a specific educational context and encourages students to reflect on it, they will not be able to adopt a rational attitude to personal and national issues. They may, in fact, leave the institution with no awareness of their role in their personal and national development. In other words, in the absence of a clear awareness of responsibilities, higher education as a social investment fails, and both the student and the state lose heavily. Most of our students have no opportunity to realise that inherent to higher education is a set of responsibilities, especially in a country like India, which offers education at a nominal price.

Critical English language education

The discussion points out the need for a critical dialogue on the politics of language in the university curriculum. I do not claim that this alone will address the conceptual thinness in our approach to English language education. But, it will certainly raise the awareness of everyone concerned in the right direction. It will also push them further to think, 'What can I do in my situation?' This is a prerequisite for formulating and reformulating socially relevant educational interventions. As Fairclough (1995, 221) observes, 'if problems of language and power are to be seriously tackled, they will be tackled by the people who are directly involved, especially the people who are subject to linguistic forms of domination and manipulation,' and their success depends upon the 'theoretical and analytical resources' they have access to. They require 'programmes of . . . critical language awareness . . . to develop the capacities of people for language critique, including their capacities for reflexive analysis of the educational process itself.' (ibid., 221). The language critique, hence, should form an essential part of the language education curriculum. How are languages and language users politically located? What is linguistic identity? How is linguistic identity related to cultural identity? What makes language a cultural tool or weapon, and how does it relate to the emotional security of an individual, society or national self-esteem? When does it become an instrument of emotional and cultural oppression? Most importantly, what is the relevance of such questions to the formulation and reformulation of context-specific pedagogical practices? It is by examining the legitimacy of our practices, through such questions, that we will be able to evolve democratic principles of legitimation (Fairclough 1989, Tollefson 1995).

There is no denying the fact that all English language education is politically constructed. Therefore, every pedagogical intervention, if it has to function as a socially relevant medium, must be accompanied by critical tools for evaluating and reformulating it, and these tools must be available to both the teacher and the learner. The greater their insights in relation to the politics of English language use, the more critical they will become of their own use of different languages including English. Therefore, it is the chief responsibility of universities to let the curriculum draw sustenance from critical enquiry into the relationship between language and society and to develop the infrastructure for encouraging the stakeholders to collaborate in this direction. The influence of social needs on the curriculum and vice versa has to be addressed by critical pedagogy which problematises and legitimates every aspect of education in its specific social context (Freire 1970, Giroux 1992, Giroux and McLaren 1994, Pennycook 1999). This is important, especially, in developing countries such as India, which have, for centuries, been the testing grounds for western ideas and the dumping grounds for outdated hardware and software, laboratory equipment and junked ships. While the harmful effects of the latter are discussed by academics and NGOs, that of the former are pondered upon by very few academics and even fewer policy makers.

Critical pedagogy (Freire 1970, Giroux and McLaren 1994, Pennycook 1999), hence, has significant implications not only for the individuals concerned but also for the world outside the classroom. The teacher and the learner must view academic activity more in terms of an awareness-raising critique whose aim is to identify the positive and negative aspects of the process of English language education. They must be pushed further to develop meaningful alternatives which can turn the various verbal and non-verbal means of education into effective instruments of self-affirmation. It will help them understand their roles as subjects of research and agents of change. The English language teacher and learner have as much responsibility to be scientific as a physics or a chemistry teacher. In fact, a clear conceptual framework of the roles of different stakeholders including the policy maker, parent, teacher, learner, material writer, examiner and employer in a higher educational context enables everyone concerned to reflect on the social relevance of higher education in English and to realise their responsibilities. Clearly, pedagogy in the context of English in countries like India has primarily two aims. It must raise the stakeholders' awareness of the political nature of their position, and initiate the process of their negotiating it to empower themselves. These aims will be realised only when the teaching/learning of languages, and particularly English, is considered to be a branch of education.

The critical educator

Education, especially higher education, demands critical educators and not just subject experts. Unlike the latter, the former realise the ever-changing nature of the components of the educational context. Language policies, educational theories, and the changing needs of a society are only a few of the components of our English language educational context, and they change from time to time. The critical pedagogist realises that the change is a result of the constant interaction between every component of the context with every other component, and the nature of this interaction has to be reflected upon in relation to the classroom within the classroom. He is sensitive to his role as an agent of change and subjects his own pedagogical practices to clinical investigation with a view to formulate those principles of language use that will help him acquire a perspective on his relationship with English, especially in the context of his identity as a self-respecting bilingual or multilingual. More importantly, the critical pedagogist is aware of the difference between research and propaganda; he adopts a clinical and intellectual approach to the issue and works towards a solution that will contribute to social harmony. In the name of research, the critical pedagogist does not embark upon a fault-finding mission which will hurt the society.

Being critical encourages the educator to examine higher education as an interactive process between the present and the future of his/her society. Also, being closest to the grassroots, the educator is a practical think-tank who guides others including policy makers, textbook writers, examiners and students. He realises that pedagogy offers him 'an opportunity to . . . move beyond the particularistic politics of class, ethnicity, race, and gender (*add language*). . . to develop a radical democratic politics that stresses difference within unity . . . Central to such a politics and pedagogy is a notion of community developed around a shared conception of social justice, rights, and entitlement. Such a notion is especially necessary at a time in our history in which the value of such concerns has been subordinated to the priorities of the market and used to legitimate the interests of the rich at the expense of the poor, the unemployed, and the homeless' (Giroux 1992, 81). It is in this context that the critical educator makes organised and consistent efforts to expand and enrich the general pool of knowledge about his specific educational context and thus, adds intellectual integrity to the whole process of education. He/she is constantly thinking, 'What should I do in my situation?' As He An E (2005, 20) observes, 'on the basis of my . . . experiences at the school, I reframed my assumptions and beliefs of ELT, and applied and tested them in my own practice. This series of actions coincided with the process of an experiential learning cycle, namely, concrete experience, observation and analysis, abstract reconceptualization, and active experimentation. Reflecting on my limited but valuable experience, I realized that the significance of the experience did not lie in the fact that I had been to the classroom, but in that I became consciously aware of the importance of teaching experience as the inspiration for ELT and teacher education.'

This shows that the critical educator approaches a piece of knowledge only as a tool of further enquiry. He/she considers every teaching experience to be an opportunity to evaluate his/her perspectives on educational interventions. In sum, the teacher in his/her role as a critical educator considers teaching to be an activity that involves a continuous scientific study of the interaction between the various components of the educational context which include his/her own role as an agent of self-affirmation, and understands that his/her research holds the key to depoliticising the process of education itself. His/her primary aim is to place the whole exercise of English language education in its sociopolitical context and evolve tools for processing its ever-changing nature in relation to the user's self-esteem and empowerment.

The critical learner

The critical language learner, especially in a multilingual country, is conscious of his/her responsibilities in the context of the relationship between language use and social context. He/she is, hence, sensitive to the fact that social, economic and political forces determine the nature of acceptance of a language and its user. This meta-consciousness is evident in his/her academic and social interactions with others, and it helps him/her play the role of a change agent. He/she tries to find answers to questions, which every democratically inclined academic should address in a multilingual society. What can he/she, as an educated and conscientious language user, contribute to the awareness that all languages are equal? What efforts should he/she make to preserve his/her linguistic and cultural heritage? What is his/her responsibility in evolving practices which help understand the nature of knowledge related to language and language learning and its relationship to pedagogical practices?

Most importantly, as a learner of English, he/she is conscious of the power of the language and uses it only to widen his/her scope of understanding. In fact, he/she considers it to be his/her responsibility to spread this awareness. This is one of the directions in which he/she contributes to a healthy balance between the use of different languages in his/her society. In other words, he/she realises that he/she is responsible for the exercise of teaching/learning English for employment not preventing his/her society from adopting a critical outlook towards the language and the culture that it brings along.

The English language learner, in India has always visualised himself in the role of a receiver. He has accepted whatever he has been told despite his awareness that most of what he has received has been imported. In the role of a critical learner, he examines the relevance of this knowledge to his own growth as a language user in a specific social context and tries to find ways to assert himself. For, he understands that his job is not just to acquire the ability to use English. It also includes the production and scrutiny of context-relevant knowledge and practices.

The critical learner steps outside of himself as a learner and subjects his own language use and language learning practices to a detailed investigation. It is only then that his learning will be rendered coherent and he will become independent as a language user- learner and his insights will become a part of his educational context. The critical learner, through this intellectual exercise, contributes not only the knowledge related to language learning but also the tools to examine this knowledge. In sum, he understands higher education as an opportunity, created for him by his society, to empower himself and the process of language education as well.

Conclusion

'English is spoken as . . . the second language by . . . 375 million speakers, . . . has official or special status in at least 75 countries with a total population of over 2 billion . . . Such staggering number of . . . users could only be taught by indigenous non-native speaker English teachers. Nevertheless, little is known about these English teachers outside their own countries. There are a number of reasons for this. The field of English language teaching—in terms of textbook publishers, journals, teacher-training programmes, and teacher organizations—is dominated by British and American interests' (Braine 2005, xii). Empowerment, in this context, would mean taking control of all these factors to create a knowledge base which will guide the second language user to negotiate his use of English in relation to his linguistic and cultural heritage. As teachers from various countries report (ibid. 2005), pedagogy holds the key to the empowerment of the individual and the society. Given the situation, the critical educator and the critical learner, especially in non-native countries, need a stimulating environment to reflect on pedagogical practices and reconceptualise and redefine English language education from a sociocultural point of view. As a first step, universities must transfer languages from the faculty of arts to the faculty of education and shift the present focus from English language oracy/literacy to English language education. It should also introduce graduate research programmes in English Language Studies to raise the non-native speaker's awareness of how the ESL curriculum contributes to identity construction. Similarly, the University Grants Commission must establish and develop centres of English language pedagogy with advanced research libraries to facilitate bilingual/multilingual stakeholders to negotiate their empowerment.

References

Agnihotri, R.K., and A.L. Khanna. 1997. *Problematizing English in India*. New Delhi: Sage Publications.

Annamalai, E.1992. Satan and Saraswati: The Double Face of English in India. In *English in India: Theoretical and Applied Issues,* ed. O.N. Koul. New Delhi: Creative.

Braine, George, ed. 2005. *Teaching English to the World: History, Curriculum, and Practice*. New Jersey: Lawrence Erlbaum.

Canagarajah, S. 2004. Subversive Identities, Pedagogical Safe Houses, and Critical Learning. In *Critical Pedagogies and Language Learning,* eds. B. Norton and K. Toohey. Cambridge: Cambridge University Press.

Cummins, J. 1996. *Negotiating Identities: Education for Empowerment in a Diverse Society*. Ontario: California Association for Bilingual Education.

Fairclough, N. 1989. *Language and Power*. London: Longman.

________. 1995. *Critical Discourse Analysis: The Critical Study of Language*. London: Longman.

Freire, P. 1970. *Pedagogy of the Oppressed*. Trans. M.B. Ramos. New York: Penguin Education.

Giroux, H. 1992. *Border Crossings: Cultural Workers and the Politics of Education*. New York: Routledge.

________ and P. McLaren, eds. 1994. *Between Borders*. London: Routledge.

He, An E. 2005 Learning and Teaching English in the People's Republic of China. In *Teaching English to the World: History, Curriculum, and Practice*, ed. G. Braine. New Jersey: Lawrence Erlbaum.

Ibrahim, Awad El Karim. M. 1999. Becoming Black: Rap and Hip-Hop, Race, Gender, Identity, and the Politics of ESL Learning. In A. Pennycook, ed., *Critical Approaches to TESOL {Special Issue} TESOL Quarterly* 33(3): 349–369.

Kachru, B., ed. 1982. *The Other Tongue: English Across Cultures*. Oxford: Pergamon.

Khubchandani, L. 1991. *Language, Culture, and Nation-Building: Challenges and Modernisation*. Shimla: Indian Institute of Advanced Studies.

Pennycook, A. 1994. *The Cultural Politics of English as an International Language*. London and New York: Longman.

________, ed. 1999. *Critical Approaches to TESOL {Special Issue} TESOL Quarterly*, 33(3).

Ram, Tulsi. 1991. English and Imperial Expansion. In *English in India: Issues and Problems*, eds. R.S. Gupta and Kapil Kapoor. Delhi: Academic Foundation.

Rampton, M.B.H. 1990. Displacing the 'Native Speaker': Expertise, Affiliation, and Inheritance. *English Language Teaching Journal* 44, 2: 97–101.

Shondel. J. N. 2005. Language, Identities and ESL Pedagogy. *Language and Education*. 19, 3: 194–211.

Skutnabb-Kangas, T. and Robert Phillipson, eds. 1994. *Linguistic Human Rights: Overcoming Linguistic Discrimination*. Berlin and New York: Mouton de Gruyter.

Tharoor, S. 2005. *Bookless in Baghdad*. New Delhi: Penguin Books India Pvt. Ltd.

Tickoo, M.L. 1994. Kashmiri, a Majority-Minority Language: An Exploratory Essay. In *Linguistic Human Rights: Overcoming Linguistic Discrimination*, eds. T. Skutnabb-Kangas and Robert Phillipson. Berlin and New York: Mouton de Gruyter.

Tollefson, J.W., ed. 1995. *Power and Inequality in Language Education*. Cambridge: Cambridge University Press.

Tollefson, J.W. 2002. *Language Policies in Education: Critical Issues*. New Jersey and London: Lawrence Erlbaum.

2

Language, Literacy Practices and English

Rama Kant Agnihotri

In this paper, I will try to outline the context in which language management must take place. I will also try to examine in some detail some of the parameters that must be kept in mind while preparing a sociolinguistic blueprint for the developing societies of SAARC countries, keeping in view, in particular, the millions of underprivileged and highly marginalised members of these societies. The question we need to confront is not so much 'What will be the future of English in SAARC countries?', but 'What will be the future of SAARC languages?' We also need to explore if English, which in the past has largely been associated with power and exploitation, can in any way function to reach out to the marginalised sections of society and empower them in ways in which they can fight the forces of exploitation. The global, social, political and economic forces that work ruthlessly and doggedly for extending and intensifying the use of English are indeed very powerful; on the other hand, the forces associated with local languages and literacy practices are weak and vulnerable. Let us then not worry so much about English. English will thrive not only in terms of its standard form but also in all its enormous variability. In fact, it may soon reach a peak that might mark the beginning of its decline with a simultaneous growth of the use of indigenous languages in some of those domains which were hitherto associated almost exclusively with English. We need to worry about how to reach it adequately to the underprivileged children just as we need to worry about how to enhance the proficiency levels of these children in their own languages. We create a 'muteness syndrome' (thanks to

Dr Apoorvanand of the University of Delhi for the phrase) among our children; they cannot articulate their feelings and thoughts in any language after they finish school. Different pieces of human multilinguality may soon fall into place if we appreciate the fact that languages thrive in each other's company and that the future of English in India is ensured in the company of, and not at the cost of, other Indian languages and literacy practices.

The context

The context, though pretty obvious, is conveniently ignored by most of us. It is a context in which the present and future importance of English in all domains of activity is constantly celebrated and cited as a fait accompli. These domains among others include education from pre-nursery to post-doctoral research, source of knowledge and cognitive growth, internet surfing, upward social and occupational mobility, and entry into the corporate world, administration, law, mass media, diplomacy, etc. In fact, there is no sector of elite formation that controls different resources and power structures that has remained untouched by English and its proponents.

The story of the arrival and consolidation of English in India is well documented now. (See, for e.g. Wadia 1954, Gokak 1964, Das Gupta 1970, Ram 1983, Kachru 1983, Howatt 1984, Viswanathan 1989, Suleri 1992, Niranjana 1993, Dasgupta 1993, Sunder Rajan 1993, Krishnaswamy and Sriraman 1994, Pennycook 1994, Agnihotri and Khanna 1994, 1995, 1997 and, Agnihotri, Khanna and Sachdev 1998 among others). The impact of the missionaries was of course much wider and deeper and keeps resurfacing in our history from time to time. Their interventions not only led to large-scale conversions, creating attractive spaces for *Hindutva* re-conversions today but also introduced a process of standardising various tribal languages in the Roman script, in particular through the Bible translations. The results in the field of education were of course far more pervasive and lasting. The establishment of English as a medium of instruction for the select few must be viewed, as Sunder Rajan (1993) suggests, against the background of the consolidation of English literature as a discipline, taking shape concurrently with the British imperialistic expansion and large-scale literary, cultural and linguistic engineering. The motives that informed what the British would explore, highlight or translate may be seen in Suleri (1992) and Niranjana (1993). Coupled with the filtration theory of the two Mills, the results of Macaulay's 'Minute on Indian Education' ripened much before even the British might have visualised. All support to Sanskrit and Arabic schools was withdrawn; the so-called vernaculars of India were dismissed as undeveloped and unworthy of imparting new ideas in science and humanities; and all knowledge, it was assumed, was available only through English. In fact, two years after the 1835 'Minute' of Macaulay, by 1837, 'language became a marker of two separate levels of social operation—the upper level reserved for English, the lower for the vernaculars. It was naively thought that a handful of people who were 'Indian in blood and colour, but English in taste, in opinions, in morals, and in intellect' will automatically have the ability to and assume the responsibility of refining and enriching the Indian 'vernaculars'. It is surprising how these scholars could forget the battles of various European vernaculars against Latin, of pre-Chaucerian English against Latin and French, and of the Prakrits from which most Indian languages emerged against Sanskrit. It should be clear that we do not first sit down to standardise a language in terms of its grammar, dictionary, etc., and then use it; in fact, we first use it extensively in all domains of activity, including, say teaching physics and mathematics, and then prepare its grammars and dictionaries. As we will soon see, such ruthless decisions are predicated on a mistaken understanding of the nature and structure of language in addition to imperialist designs.

In any case, the persistent consolidation of English added a new dimension to the Indian patriarchic society, which was already severely stratified along several axis, including caste, territorial segregation, gender and class. If at all there was any hope for the restoration of such values as freedom, justice and liberty in a free India, it was to that extent made more difficult. There are of course constitutional provisions for the scheduled castes, scheduled tribes and other backward castes, yet it is absolutely necessary that they acquire a reasonable level of proficiency in English, often at the cost of their native languages, if they wish to get decent jobs. We also know that most people in these categories who manage to do well may not always come from among the poorest in their respective categories. All this eventually leads to a kind of alienation from their own community; the community, in general, stays where it was. Bidwai (2004) was stunned to discover that among the 300 journalists of the *Times of India* group of newspapers, there was not a single dalit and only three OBCs, and he wondered how the *savarnas,* constituting only a tenth of the population, could have nine-tenth of its merit; and still worse, how could most people think that it was natural and spontaneous and that there wasn't much that could be done about it. As Ngugi Wa Thiong'o (1986, 39) said, 'We must distance ourselves from the false and bloody logic of development theory handed to us by imperialism; the claim that the cleanliness of one person must depend on pouring dirt onto others; that the health of a few must depend on their passing their leprosy onto others; that the wealth of a few nations must be rooted in the poverty of the masses of people and nations.'

It is becoming increasingly clear that the future industry, particularly the service industry, including call centres and BPOs, is going to require a huge manpower with fairly high levels of proficiency in oral and written English and that this need cannot be met by the English medium schools alone. 'The Indian IT sector also plans to explore the high-end Knowledge-based Process Outsourcing (KPO) as global corporations move BPO, KPO and other comparable work such as intellectual property research to offshore locations. The new KPOs comprise companies providing higher-end research and analytical services to overseas clients in a wide spectrum of business areas. These include basic data research, integration and management, market research, equity research, engineering design, animation and simulation, medical content and services, remote education and publishing. Other areas with significant latent potential for KPO include pharmaceuticals, biotechnology, legal support, intellectual property research, and design and development for automotive and aerospace industries' (www.indiadaily.com). According to the National Association of Software and Service Companies (Nasscom), the total market size of KPO business in India may rise to a staggering $15.5 billion from the present $1.2 billion. The magnitude of person power needed by the service sector will in no way be met by the present English-medium public school system alone. Several BPOs and KPOs are looking towards the government school and college system to provide them person power with adequate control on English, particularly spoken English (the demand for 'voice' and accent trainers is multiplying by the day).

We need not deny the many advantages that have accrued to us due to English; indeed its role as a tool to acquire knowledge and read other literatures in translation, its role in education and its being a window to the world cannot be denied. Perhaps in tomorrow's India everybody must acquire a fairly high level of proficiency in English. But how do we ensure that that level of English reaches everyone and how do we ensure that the native languages of these people are not damaged in the process. We, therefore, need to carefully rethink not only about our language and educational policies but also and more importantly about our economic and political policies. The educational and linguistic planning can only be a subcomponent, though of course an extremely important one, of the overall sociopolitical and economic vision. The present paper only suggests some of the parameters along which the future language policy component of this blueprint could be designed.

Language

If we really wish to understand what the future place of English in India should be, we should carefully re-examine what we mean by the word 'language' itself. It will not do to simply say that language is an important means of communication. One of the foremost contributions of modern linguistics has been to emphatically show the structural equality of all languages, thereby neutralising the sociopolitical distinctions that are made between language, dialect, variety, mixed code, etc. More certainly than ever before we now have reasons to believe that all languages including the so-called mixed codes that surface all the time in human interaction are rulegoverned at the phonological, morphological and syntactic levels and that all human beings are endowed with an innate capacity to acquire not just one, but several languages. It seems that there is an underlying universal grammar that constrains all possible languages. Formal linguistic theory and analysis have focused on 'a language', in the sense of 'an object out there' or as embedded in the neurological system of the human brain, in terms of pairing a lexicon and a set of syntactic rules to create meaning (see studies such as those reported in Geirsson and Losonsky 1996). At this level of language faculty, all humans are equal, so designed by nature. As Sapir (1921, 234) puts it, 'When it comes to linguistic form, Plato walks with the Macedonian swineherd, Confucius with the head-hunting savage of Assam.'

Sociolinguistic theory and practice, on the other hand, have focused on the more dynamic and human aspects of language; they have shown that language is much more than just a formal object. It is closely, and in extremely complex and unpredictable ways, associated with our thoughts: it defines the limits of our thought, it is one of the most potent symbolic systems representing our emotions and ideas, and it is closely associated with socioeconomic and political power being often used as a powerful tool for social exploitation (Wittgenstein 1953). Finally, all individuals control a range of variable linguistic behaviour, modulating it sensitively in relation to person, place and topic. Multilinguality is an essential part of an individual's identity and in this respect all human beings share the same platform. In this overarching multilinguality, we need to subsume not only the existence of a multiplicity of languages but also a whole range of literacy practices, oral and written, as well as a variety of modulations of performing arts and their intricate combinations.

Multilingualism

All the South Asian countries are multilingual both at the individual and the societal levels. It is indeed one of the most significant features that bind countries like Bhutan, Bangladesh, India, Maldives, Nepal, Sri Lanka and Pakistan together. This togetherness subsumes a whole range of oral tradition and literacy practices across different forms of cultures and different strata of society. According to the SIL (2002) Ethnologue database, a small country like Nepal uses 121 languages. It has two official languages, Nepali and Gurung, but languages belonging to such diverse language families as Indo-Aryan, Tibeto-Burman and Austro-Asiatic families are spoken by a sizeable number of speakers. The situation in other countries such as Sri Lanka, Bangladesh, Pakistan and India is not very different. Though a small island, Sri Lanka uses 8 languages. These include the Indo-Aryan Sinhala, the official language, Indo-European English, Dravidian Tamil, Indo-Aryan Veddah and two creoles, one Portuguese based and the other Malay based. In Bangladesh, once again, several Tibeto-Burman, Indo-Aryan and Austro-Asiatic languages are spoken. There are over 38 languages used in Bangladesh including Bengali, Chittagonian, Sylhetti, Santali, Sadri, Meitei, Khasi, Garo and Arakanese among others. Pakistan uses 69 languages and has three national or official languages, namely, Urdu, Sindhi and English. As in other South Asian countries, languages belonging to the Indo-Aryan, Dravidian and Tibeto-Burman families are spoken by a substantial number of speakers here. A sizeable number of people (over 55,000) also speak Burushaski, a language isolate (see SIL 2002).

However, the paradigm example of multilingualism beyond doubt is indeed India. In spite of Grierson's remarkable *Linguistic Survey of India* and several census surveys, it has not been possible to exactly determine the number of languages spoken in India. This must really be the case with all multilingual countries for what is counted as a language (and not, for example, as a dialect or a pidgin or a mixed code) is not a neutral linguistic question. It is decided by a variety of social, historical and ideological factors. According to the 1961 census, India had 1,652 languages belonging to five different language families: Indo-Aryan, Dravidian, Tibeto-Burman, Austro-Asiatic and Andamanese; it also indicated that 87 languages were used in the print media, 71 on the radio and 41 in schools. The 1991 census showed that there were 10,400 mother tongues used by the people of India. Through a sustained exercise of 'thorough linguistic scrutiny, editing and rationalization', these mother tongues were reduced to just 216 and of these, 85 were subsumed under the 18 scheduled languages of the constitution. Major languages, often with long histories and a respectable literary tradition, such as Awadhi, Bhojpuri, Bundeli, Chattisgarhi, Maghai, Mewari, Rajasthani, etc. (in all, over 50 languages), were subsumed under the rubric of Hindi. Bhojpuri alone is claimed as a mother tongue by over 23,000,000 people. In fact, languages like Awadhi and Bhojpuri should be treated as the parents rather than the dialects of Hindi. For example, it is not just that Tulsidas's

(1534–1623 A.D.) famous rendering of the story of Ram and Sita in the *Ramcaritmanas* is not in Sanskrit or Hindi but in Awadhi, but that there is an extremely rich and vibrant oral and literary tradition in the Awadhi region even today. The multilingual fabric of India as of other countries is sustained by functional differentiation as well as continuous convergence of different languages. It is not just in metropolitan cities such as Mumbai, Chennai, Delhi or Kolkata or in their ever-multiplying urban slums that we find rich and complex multilingual behaviour; even a remote village in Himachal, Kerala, Manipur or. Gujarat uses several languages simultaneously. A school boy in the small town Mandi of Himachal Pradesh in the north, may speak Mandayali at home, Hindi and English at school and a mixed variety among his friends. Such variability in linguistic behaviour, as Pandit (1969; 1972) argues, facilitates rather than obstructs communication. Domains of behaviour have to be seen on a linguistic continuum. At the extremes of these domains, linguistic behaviour may display stability and language differentiation, i.e., each extreme may be associated with an identifiable stable language in terms of structure and norms but in the areas where these domains flow into each other, linguistic behaviour may be far less stable and normative and may be characterised by code mixing, code switching, convergence and the emergence of new languages. The norm in India, as perhaps in the whole of the South Asian region, is language maintenance rather than language loss though very few of the languages in each country may have written forms. In the relatively isolated tribal ethnic groups, the rate of bilingualism is higher than in other communities and despite the absence of political and institutional support, these languages have not only survived but also developed several lingua francas. In some cases, it is perhaps true that languages die. In Pakistan, all the 69 languages are living; in Sri Lanka, only one language, Pali, is extinct; in Nepal, of the 121 languages, only Kusunda, is extinct (see SIL 2002). SIL lists 398 languages in India, of which it seems 11 are extinct. However, what is not noted in such surveys is the fact that even as some languages disappear, new ones are created and the overall architecture of the multilingual society is preserved. The emergence of new mixed codes in several Indian urban cities is now well attested. Apparently even in the Andaman region, the incidence of inter-marriage among different groups such as the Aka-Kol or Aka-Bea marrying into the Aka-Jeru group is very high and the children born of such marriages speak mixed languages (Anvita Abbi, pers. commu.). As established in Agnihotri (2001), even though India was divided into federal units on the basis of language, there is not a single unit that may legitimately be called monolingual. In several states such as Andhra Pradesh in the south, Haryana in the north, West Bengal in the east, Maharashtra in the west and Uttar Pradesh in central India, all the 18 scheduled languages are represented. The linguistic diversity is paralleled by a diversity in scripts, though all of them perhaps originate from the Brahmi script. India uses 25 scripts (Singh and Manoharan 1993, 28) and several educated people use more than one script.

This, of course, does not license any romanticisation of multilingualism in SAARC countries. The political dimensions are indeed forbidding. The major threat comes from English, which though a very small part of the multilingual situation appropriates a completely disproportionate portion of the economic resources and social power, perhaps more so in India than anywhere else. The route to decent education and employment is almost exclusively through English and the number of children who grow up having only marginal control on different languages including their mother tongues is multiplying. A critical awareness about language and powers associated with it is essential for democracy (see Fairclough 1989; 1992).

This multilinguality subsumes, as said above, not only the oral but also the written and the performative including an intense dialogic interaction among them. It is extremely difficult to draw clear boundaries between them. The moment we try to say that here the oral or the performative ends and the written begins, we get into serious problems. Consider, for example, the dynamics of all the three in the reading, recitation and performance of the *Ramayana*, not just in a variety of languages in India but also in Nepal, Myanmar, Malayasia, Indonesia, Thailand, Laos, Sri Lanka, etc., (see Raghavan 1980; Iyengar 1983). According to Singh (1997, 2000), despite their own credentials to the contrary, several linguists continue to build theories of language grounded in monolinguality. Multilinguality is constitutive of human existence, and truth, freedom and justice are its defining predicates.

Literacy practices

When we talk of multilingualism, its advantages and the threats it faces from homogenising forces, we also need to think about a whole range of literacy practices, oral or written. Several studies reported in Street (2001), including, among others, Dyer and Choksi on the literacy, schooling and development among Indian Rabari nomads, Priti Chopra on the problems of conducting ethnographic research in a North Indian village, Bryan Maddox on literacy and market in Bangladesh, Shirin Zubair on literacy and gender in Pakistan, and Robinson-Pant on women's health and literacy in Nepal have at least two things in common. They show that the secular and autonomous models of literacy have not paid any dividends and that we need to think in terms of situated literacy practices, which may encompass a variety of symbolic systems central to the existence of a given community. What is most unfortunate is that secular perspectives on literacy conceptualise it in a minimal way. Across the developing world, where literacy levels are extremely low, a farcical distinction is made between education and literacy (Agnihotri 2002a), and literacy is measured in terms of Minimum Levels of Learning (MLL) or just the ability to count till hundred and the ability to read a few words and write one's name. Such a view of literacy is indeed an insult to human intelligence. The consequences of teaching languages including English from such a perspective are far too obvious to be documented here; even after ten to twelve years of education in two or three languages, children acquire extremely low levels of language proficiency. Minimal literacy is believed to solve all problems. A strong correlation is seen between poverty, disease, underdevelopment and illiteracy, and it is assumed that the growth of minimal literacy will automatically solve all problems. That this can never be so should be clear from the case of Sri Lanka where though the literacy is above 87% (SIL 2002), the levels of poverty are very high, and there is hardly any industrial development. Literacy programmes in all the South Asian countries, such as India, Nepal, Bangladesh, Sri Lanka and Pakistan, generally assume that illiteracy is the root cause of all evil and that universalisation of minimal literacy will automatically solve all problems. For example, according to the UNESCO report on Bangladesh (1984, 3), 'overwhelming illiteracy is the most formidable obstacle to the modernization process'. In the case of India, we are told, 'literacy is an essential prerequisite as well as an obligation of a democratic government for bringing about large scale and informed participation of people in the process of democratic functioning of the Government and decentralization of tasks and responsibilities' (UNESCO 1984b: 33). But that literacy will consist at best of making people 'read with understanding road signs, posters, simple instructions, newspapers for neo-literates, etc.', 'writing independently short letters, applications, filling up cheques, forms, etc.' and having some 'idea of percentage, interest, proportion and area *not involving fractions*. . .' (ibid., 24–25, emphasis mine). How can people with such abysmally low levels of literacy actively and critically participate in a democracy and take on responsibilities?

It should not surprise anyone that literacy levels in South Asia remain so low in spite of all the national and international noise that is made in the name of 'education for all'. Nobody is really serious about the issue. The budgetary allocation for education rarely exceeds 5–6%. Those in power never really wish that the masses should get access to the knowledge that ensures their control on social institutions. The literacy programmes and schools (which in the case of poor children will rarely have either teachers or rooms or books) completely ignore the languages, literacy practices and cultures of the young learners there. When in 1859, the then prime minister of the Rana regime opened several vernacular schools for the children of Nepal, he was promptly dismissed and all the schools were closed. In 1951, Nepal had only 11 secondary schools and only 2% of its population was literate (UNESCO 1984b). Even in the case of India, where tall claims are made in connection with literacy, the 1991 census showed that the literacy rate in the seven-plus age group was only 52%, while female literacy was 39%, rural literacy 45% and the dropout rate from class 1 to class 5 approximately 50% (National Institute of Adult Education 1993). This indeed is a dismal picture. According to the SIL (2002) estimates, the literacy rate is 25% in Bangladesh, 29% in Nepal, 26% in Pakistan and 52% in India. The orality, literacy and education debate provides a space where we can re-examine the whole issue afresh. Lankshear (1987, 216) makes a distinction between proper and improper literacies where proper literacy comprises education that enables people to make rational judgements, 'enabling them to identify, understand and act to transform social relations and practices in which power is structured unequally'. Sustaining local literacies and oral traditions must thus be an integral part of proper literacy (see Agnihotri 1994; Barton 1994; Street 1994).

In the 'cognitive and cultural' perspective on literacy, oral societies are generally regarded rather primitive so far cognitive skills and cultural sophistication are concerned. In the case of literate societies, fairly high levels of education in the modern sense are subsumed, and it is often argued that the kind of abstract and complex knowledge that is possible in such literate societies is almost inconceivable in oral societies. Among others, scholars such as Ong (1967), Goody (1968) and Oxenham (1980), have associated empirical analysis, logical thinking and sustained reflective introspection with the invention of script literacy by the Greeks. The cognitively rich oral traditions, such as the ancient Indian Vedic tradition, pose a serious problem for such a view of orality and literacy. The Vedic texts are said to have all those features that are generally associated exclusively with writing, including technical information, moral judgement, universal definition, Kantian imperative, mathematical relationship, epistemology and logic (cf. Havelock 1963), and we know for sure that for centuries these texts have been orally transmitted.

It would appear that the divide between orality and literacy and also that between the two perspectives on their relationship is untenable and is only sociopolitically motivated. The oral and the written, like the verbal and the graphic or like dance and sculpture, constantly flow into each other. In the pedagogical perspective, it is difficult to understand why states, which consider 'education for all' their constitutional responsibility, should at all make a distinction between education and literacy, where education is clearly for the rich and literacy for the underprivileged. Similarly, in the cognitive perspective, it is difficult to understand why scholars who constantly harp on the specific intellectual abilities associated with writing do not see the dynamic relationship between orality and literacy and their complementarity. Denny (1991) has argued that orality and literacy cannot be distinguished on the basis of logic, and abstract and rational thought; they can only be distinguished to some extent on the basis of contextualisation and differentiation. Even in terms of language acquisition, Vygotsky (1978) shows how children develop their own systems of writing much before they start speaking coherently. The dots and lines they make at specific points of a piece of paper often represent for them the characters and events of the verbal stories they have heard from their parents.

Conclusion

It appears then that we are in a trap—a formidable one. There is no running away from English, and there is no way we can afford to sacrifice our multilinguality and our unique identities. Several states in India have already introduced English from class 1; that may help address the needs of the global market, but if we do not do a good job in terms of materials, teachers, classroom transaction, teacher-training, infrastructure, etc., in addition to introducing a large number of other processes of social transformation, the societal divisions between the rich and the poor may persist. There is, however, as always a lesson to be learnt from history. Whenever the tyranny of a classical language, be it Greek, Latin or Sanskrit, became suffocating, the so-called vernaculars, whether in the East or the West, asserted their unique voice and won the battle with distinction. Postmodernist thought has brought out the significance of the local more powerfully than ever before, although, given our poverty and the nature of our hierarchical societies, we cannot afford the luxury of the postmodernist rejection of the enlightenment rationality, and welcome its 'tolerant indifference' and 'happy nihilism'. We constantly need to take recourse to rationality (Nanda 2001) if we have to disentangle ourselves from the kind of stereotypes and political manoeuvring we are constantly subjected to. What we need is careful language planning preceded by rigorous sociolinguistic surveys involving elicitation and analysis of language choice, frequency and competence; respect for multilingualism and multiple identities; insistence on higher budgetary allocations for the welfare sector; more serious thought on the philosophical and epistemological aspects of education, examination of the dichotomy drawn between education and minimal literacy; proactive planning, affirmative action and engagement in long term collaboration with a network of serious and motivated NGOs within and across

SAARC and other countries. The site for experimenting with these aspects of multilinguality is the classroom, the formal or the non-formal. In this site, the teacher is also a learner, and messages are transacted in multiple literacies. Intertextuality, translation, exposure to different kinds of genre, engagement with the basic cognitive exercise of data elicitation, classification and categorisation, freedom to raise questions without fear, interdisciplinarity and the ability to use modern technology would inform this new space, of which English will only be one part. At the moment it is said that over 80% of computer-based communication is in English; there are enough reasons to believe that it will fall to 40% in the next decade (Graddol 1997, 61). The very same technology that has ensured the increasing dominance of English, along with several other parallel processes outlined above, will help us elevate the status of other languages and literacy practices, and rationally minimise the role of English in a new world order.

References

Agnihotri, R.K. 1994. Campaign-based Literacy Programmes: The Case of the Ambedkar Nagar Experiment in Delhi. In Barton, D. ed., 47–56.

————————. 1995. *English Language Teaching in India: Issues and Innovations*. New Delhi: Sage Publications.

————————. 2001. English in Indian Education. In *Language Education in Multilingual India*, ed. C.J. Daswani. New Delhi: UNESCO.

————————. 2002. A Farce Called Literacy. In *Practice and Research in Literacy*, eds. A. Mukherjee, and D. Vasantha. New Delhi: Sage Publications.

———————— and A.L Khanna. 1994. Second Language Acquisition: Socio-Cultural and Linguistic Aspects of English in India. New Delhi: Sage Publications.

———————— and A.L. Khanna. 1997. The Social Psychological Perspective on Second Language Learning: A Critique. In *Grammar, Language, and Society*, ed. R. Singh. New Delhi: Sage Publications.

__________, A. L. Khanna, and I. Sachdev, eds. 1998. *Research in Applied Linguistics Vol. 4: Social Psychological Perspectives on Second Language Learning*. New Delhi: Sage Publications.

Barton, D., ed. 1994. Sustaining Local Literacies. (Special Issue of *Language and Education 8*).

Bidwai, P. 2004. India is Marked by Cascading Inequalities. *The Radical Humanist* 68 6: 15–16.

Census of India. 1961 and 1991. New Delhi: Registrar General and Census Commissioner, India.

Das Gupta, J. 1970. *Language Conflict and National Development*. Bombay: Oxford University Press.

Dasgupta, P. 1993. *The Otherness of English: India's Auntie Tongue Syndrome*. New Delhi: Sage Publications.

Denny, J. 1991. Rational Thought in Oral Culture and Literate Decontextualisation. In *Literacy and Orality*, eds. D. Olson and N. Torrance. Cambridge: Cambridge University Press.

Fairclough, N. 1989. *Language and Power*. London: Longman.

——————, ed. 1992. *Critical Language Awareness*. London: Longman.

Geirsson, H. and M. Losonky, eds. 1996. *Readings in Language and Mind*. Cambridge, MA: Blackwell Publishing.

Gokak, V. K. 1964. *English in India: Its Present and Future*. Bombay: Asia Publishing House.

Goody, J., ed. 1968. *Literacy in Traditional Societies*. Cambridge: Cambridge University Press.

Graddol, D. 1997. *The Future of English?* London: British Council.

Gupta, R.S. and K.S. Agarwal, eds. 1998. *Studies in Indian Sociolinguistics*. New Delhi: Creative.

Havelock, E.A. 1963. *Preface to Plato*. Cambridge, MA: Cambridge University Press.

Iyengar, K.R. Srinivasa, ed. 1983. *Asian Variations in Ramayana*. New Delhi: Sahitya Akademi.

Kachru, B.B. 1983. *Indianization of English: The English Language in India*. Delhi: Oxford University Press.

Krishnaswamy, N. and T. Sriraman, 1994. *English Teaching in India*. Madras: T.R. Publications.

Kumar, N. ed. 1994. *Women as Subjects: South Asian Histories*. New Delhi: Stree.

Lankshear, C. 1987. *Literacy, Schooling and Revolution*. London: Falmer Press.

Nanda, M. 2001. *Breaking the Spell of Dharma: Case for Indian Enlightenment*. EPW XXXVI No 27: 2551–2566.

National Institute of Adult Education. 1993. *Statistical Database for Literacy*. New Delhi.

Niranjana, T. 1993. *Siting Translation: History, Post-structuralism and the Colonial Context*. Berkeley: University of California Press.

Ong, W.J. 1967. *Orality and Literacy*. London: Methuen.

Oxenham, J. 1980. *Literacy: Writing, Reading and Social Organization*. London: Routledge and Kegan Paul.

Pandit, P.B. 1969. Parameters of Speech Variation in an Indian Community. In A. Poddar, ed. *Language and Society in India*. Shimla: Indian Institute of Advanced Studies.

——————— . 1972. India as a Sociolinguistic Area. (Gune Memorial Lectures). Pune: University of Poona.

Pennycook, A. 1994. *The Cultural Politics of English as an International Language*. London and New York: Longman.

Raghavan, V., ed. 1980. *The Ramayana Tradition in Asia*. New Delhi: Sahitya Akademi.

Ram, Tulsi. 1983. *Trading in Language: The Story of English in India*. Delhi: GDK Publications.

Sapir, E. 1921. *Language: An Introduction to the Study of Language.* New York: Harcourt Brace.

SIL International. 2002. Ethnologue: Languages of the World, 14th edition. Ethnologue Website.

Singh, K.S. and S. Manoharan. 1993. *People of India, Vol IX: Languages and Scripts*. Delhi: Anthropological Survey of India and Oxford University Press.

Singh, R. 1996. *Lectures against Sociolinguistics*. New York: Peter Lang.

———————. 2000. Chasing Butterflies in a Multilingual Garden: Grounding Even Linguistic Form in Multilinguality. *The R.N. Srivastava Memorial Lecture,* University of Delhi, Delhi.

Street, B. 1994. What is Meant by Local Literacies? In Barton, D. ed., 19–30.

——————— . 2001. ed. *Literacy and Development*. London and New York: Routledge

Suleri, S. 1992. *The Rhetoric of English in India*. Chicago: The University of Chicago Press.

Sunder Rajan, R., ed. 1993. *The Lie of the Land: English Literary Studies in India*. Delhi: Oxford University Press.

UNESCO. 1984. *Literacy Situation in Asia and the Pacific: Bangladesh*. Bangkok: Regional Office for Education in Asia and the Pacific.

UNESCO. 1984b. *Literacy Situation in Asia and the Pacific: Nepal*. Bangkok: Regional Office for Education in Asia and the Pacific.

Viswanathan, G. 1989. *Masks of Conquest: Literary Study and British Rule in India*. New York: Columbia University Press.

Vygotsky, L.S. 1978. *Mind in Society: The Development of Higher Psychological Processes*. Eds. M. Cole, et al. Cambridge, MA: Harvard University Press.

Wadia, A.R. 1954. *The Future of English in India*. Bombay: Asia Publishing House.

Wittgenstein, L. 1953. *Philosophical Investigations*. Oxford: Blackwell.

Wa Thiong'o, Ngugi 1986. *Decolonising the Mind: The Politics of Language in African Literature*. London: James Currey.

3

Language Planning Scholarship: Towards Adequacy

Thiru Kandiah

In the manifest incapacity of language and language-education planning scholarship to retrieve itself from what appears to be congenital limitations, we need to turn to a non-linguist, Ahmad (1992, 5–7), whose writings on literary postcoloniality point towards directions which even planning metatheory might usefully follow in an effort to productively reconstitute itself. In a way that would ensure the retrieval of the activity involved from the fluid world of discoursal hermeneutics into which postmodernist planning scholars would shunt it, this would entail embedding it firmly and concretely in the sociohistorically constituted 'world of political and economic realities which surround and saturate' it, understood not in the narrowing terms of historicism but with sensitivity to their varied nature and the multirhythmic processuality of their formation and workings. Such realities constitute 'the material coordinates of its production' and 'objectively determine' it, through a 'determinate set of mediations' which 'connect' the two. They would do so by defining 'the givenness of the circumstances under which individuals make their choices, their lives, their histories', that is, in ways that, rather than entrapping the individual, reflect the 'dialectic between objective determination and individual agency'.

At its most encompassing, that world of realities is the current, inexorably interlocked global order outside of which no country can viably set itself. Constituted over the past few centuries by the structuring operations of capitalism riding on an ever-renewing project of empire, it emerged as a unity, be it a contradictory unity. It was a unity organised, through all of its contradictoriness, in terms of certain typical hierarchised distributions of economic, political and social roles, functions, positions and relations, and certain typical distributions of resources, accessibility, power, and so on, on lines determined considerably by capitalism's primary mode of production. Its local, as distinct from global, theatre was the nation state, under the leadership of an emerging national bourgeoisie, which—allocated the role of functionaries of the order by the structuring operations—discharged that role either coercively or, under the more commonly prevalent democratic dispensation, by Gramscian consensual means.

The overriding task which Sri Lanka faced under these circumstances as it moved towards independence and beyond was that of postcolonial recovery and reconstruction (see Kandiah 2003, and also, 1984, 1995, 2000, 2004, for a fuller specification of some of the matters to be dealt with below). This was directed towards the restitution of subjectivity, agency and identity to the country and its people, by freeing them from the structural inequalities by means of which they had been dispossessed by empire/capitalism; and, through all of this, towards wresting for them genuine participation within the global order on a footing of equality and dignity. Necessarily anti-imperialist and egalitarian in ideological thrust, the task involved, among many other things, a restoration to centre stage of the traditional cultures that had been marginalised during the preceding several centuries and, also, the pursuit of material development (including modernisation). This development was, however, conceived not in the terms conventionally dictated from the erstwhile colonial centre but considerably in terms of such matters as the need to uplift the material living standards of the citizenry, a majority of whom had earlier been subjected to varying conditions of deprivation.

Considered only from the point of view of language, both the indigenous languages and the erstwhile colonial language, English, would quite evidently take on positions of significance within the situation. What would be less evident is that the nature of this significance can hardly be grasped by the formula of (as simple-minded and distorting as it is modish) indigenous languages for culture and identity, and English for development and modernisation. The kind of dialectical reorganisation of a colonised society that its complex history causes to take place (Fanon 1968, 210–232) had resulted, in the Lankan case, in a productive and creative interaction between the ever-present and ever-changing traditional factors of the context and the massively different material and non-material factors associated with modernity, which the country had made its own during colonial times. As far as language went, this issued in the organic mutual involvement, not necessarily in smoothly integrative ways, of all of the languages with each other within the experienced life of the country and its people, at all levels—material, ontological, existential, epistemological, ideological, and so on. Thus, the indigenous languages were by no means separate from any of the dimensions of the reconstructive tasks specified in the preceding paragraph. Similarly, in spite of the fact that English continued to be confined to a small, if expanding, minority, its role could not be described in the uncomprehending and confining philistinist and utilitarian terms conventionally drawn on in talking of 'languages of wider communication'. Many other things apart (including its interesting forms of embeddedness in the overall experience of more than just the English speaking), the notion of participation in the global order alone, understood not mechanistically, but in the more complex and organic terms outlined in Kandiah (1995), guaranteed that.

This broad situation that the material realities of the context point towards was, however, immensely complicated by other, equally sociohistorically constituted complexities and, in fact, contradictions, that also marked these realities.[1] Many of them can be identified by considering the nature of the indigenous bourgeois leadership on whom the task of recovery and reconstruction most

[1]The presidential elections of November 2005 have added a dimension to Lankan politics which make it very difficult to predict how the country will move with regard to the kinds of issues set down in the interpretive account of the situation provided in this paper. At these elections, the dominant, feudally complexioned bourgeois leadership, of whatever political stripe, that had by various strategies hitherto remained quite self-assuredly and even complacently at the undisputed helm of affairs were surprised into a kind of no-person's-land by a coalition of totally contradictory forces. Led from out of an until then low-profiled but carefully nurtured quarter of the bourgeoisie, it ranged from the progressive and

directly seemed to devolve. In the early decades, this leadership was almost entirely petit bourgeois and bilingual (in English and, at varying levels of competence, an indigenous language). English was a primary linguistic marker of the class, securing status and privilege for it, something which, in fact, never changed even when, subsequently, it reconstituted itself in a highly nationalistic image. At the same time, in spite of the very many dimensions of modernity that they had made very much their own, and the formally modern democratic situation they belonged within, the leadership (as well as a lot of the citizenry) were, from the beginning, as they have implacably continued to be, very feudal in outlook and behaviour (see Jiggins 1979, for an account of the fundamentally caste- and family-driven nature of Lankan politics), and very susceptible to issues of race, caste and religion.

This fed directly into a further characteristic which the leadership shared with all such leaderships—a fixation on their own position and power. The fact that the country had received universal franchise well ahead of the other countries of the region (as well as of the Southeast Asian region) assumed great significance in this respect. It led the leadership to see very early that, within the fundamentally multiethnic, multilinguistic, multireligious, and also unequal polity that the country had inherited from history, the parliamentary, democratic political system the former rulers had bestowed on them, along with the franchise, provided for them immense opportunities to mobilise the mass bases of support among the people by offering to satisfy their various concerns. This they readily did, through appeals of a national, reconstructionist type to issues of identity, language, culture, race, religion, and so on, and of a progressive, socialistic type to issues of the provision and equalisation of economic resources and opportunities, and of social mobility. All of these issues, needless to say, had necessary salience to the realisation of the postcolonial liberatory and egalitarian impulses and, therefore, received ready endorsement from the people.

---

democratic to the unapologetically reactionary, theocratic, chauvinist and fascist, but was held together by an overwhelming appeal to the populist impulse. How the impossible contradictions it incorporates will play out is as yet far from certain.

At the same time, driven by the need to ensure that they remained in hegemonic control of the polity, the use by the leadership of these genuinely popular concerns was populist in the sense in which Matterlart (1983) and Siegelaub (1983) use the term. That is to say, the concerns were opportunistically exploited by the leadership to serve not the people's interests, but their own classed ones. This involved considerably the use of particularly the linguistico-cultural concerns in exclusivising, majoritarian, near-theocratic (in the case of religion), and even genocidal or fascistic ways which yielded considerable political and material advantages in the struggles against their various rivals. These rivals were primarily those who could be defined in ethno-linguistic-religious terms, but included also those within the same linguistico-cultural or even ideological camp. This last-mentioned matter meant in real terms that any efforts from within the hegemonic group to address the crises created by undesirable appeals to national identity, race, religion, and so on, would invariably be thwarted, since whichever segment initiated the effort would have itself been discredited by its rivals through the use of exactly those appeals. This further meant that each significant segment had necessarily and constantly to keep looking sympathetically over its shoulder towards undesirable attitudes in case its rivals stole a march on them in this manner. And the leadership of the losers-out in the situation, including the minorities, while resisting all of this, tended to retaliate from the spaces of dispossession to which they had been consigned in very much the same coin.

A lot of this involved also the promotion in Sri Lanka of anti-English sentiments, in earlier years considerably for its imperialist, anti-national associations, and throughout for its classed nature. But, given the ways, just alluded to, in which the dialectical workings of history had positioned English within the material realities of the situation, there was simply no viable way in which those sentiments could be pushed through to their logical conclusion. In any event, even those among the leadership who, under the imperatives of their populist politics, were the most ready to promote those sentiments were acutely aware of the hegemonic privileges their own possession of it had earned (and would continue to earn) them. Whatever their public stance might have been, they were not going to take any measures relating to the language that would substantively affect these privileges. This did not change much even after the old English-dominant anglophile elite in the class had been 'put in their place' or nationalistically transformed or joined or replaced by a new, indigenous-language-dominant nationalistic elite. The complicity with English and what it stood for that this promoted was immeasurably reinforced when, just as the heady excitement of the earlier anti-English initiatives was beginning to wane somewhat, the interpellations of global capitalism/empire to the bourgeois leadership began to become increasingly louder and more insistent, through pressures exerted by the then colossally growing phenomenon of globalisation, accompanied by the transnationalisation of capital, reminding them of the roles that had been appointed to them by its structuring operations. Their responses were so compliant that the role of English, as the first language of the global order, began to be increasingly reinforced in language education planning, even at the expense of some of the egalitarian nationalist measures taken earlier and of their beneficiaries. Interestingly, this took place regardless of publicly professed ideological–political differences, including those relating to issues of nationalism and socialism, among successive governments. All of this also meant that the leadership which presided over the destiny of the country as it moved on operated a great deal of the time on the basis of commitments to positions which were irreconcilable with each other.

The account just concluded of the 'material coordinates' of the language and language-education planning measures, practices and accompanying attitudes reveals how very complicated and even ambivalent and contradictory the 'world of political and economic realities which surround and saturate' them is. The very reasonable conclusion that the ambivalences and contradictions of the measures, practices and attitudes are then but a reflex of the ambivalences and contradictions of the material coordinates can be very easily confirmed by a demonstration that every single one of the former can be explained by reference to many of the latter.

Consider, for instance, the problems of explanation raised for current approaches to planning by the less than satisfactory pedagogical practice that planning decisions cause to be adopted as well as persisted within Lankan ELT classrooms, especially the dependence of this practice on imported packages of pre-determined methods, techniques, and so on, that often are not cognizant of or sensitive to the specificities of the context in which they are required to be applied.

Against the background of the account of the material realities provided above, this can be seen as a manifestation of a commitment within the local ELT field to what Yeatman (1990, 18), dealing with the 'discourse of management' within the field of administration, terms 'managerialist rationality'. It is a rationality that on the one hand facilitates 'more democratic and less discriminatory' practice than that which prevailed earlier, operating on the basis of a 'construction of "merit" ' that affords a place to negotiation, self-motivation, and so on, among those involved. Roughly corresponding with such emphases in the current global ELT world would be its concern with matters like learner-centredness, human rights, and also multiculturalism, unity and ethnic harmony.

The approach of managerialist rationality to the specification of 'merit', however, is a 'highly normative and prescriptive' one, 'shaped by requirements of management in private sector firms' and responsive primarily to the concerns of 'the executive levels of (the managerial) line command' . . . 'Geared to the achievement of operational goals' and 'outcomes' and fundamentally instrumental in orientation, it is a reductive results-oriented, task-centred approach, which remains 'context-indifferent' and 'insulated from the demands and complexity of its environment', and 'provides no place to "people" and "process" emphases' which remain mindful of 'substantive' matters of society, philosophy and ethics related to the issue of 'the good society'. Less concerned, therefore, with substantive content and knowledge than with information, it instead shows an overriding preoccupation with outcome directed technique(s), methods, procedures and skills as such, valorising them over fundamental thinking and understanding and, even, 'fetishising' them. An important aspect of the approach is the phenomenon of 'credentialism', a preoccupation with the acquisition of credentials or qualifications which attest to their holders' 'merit', assessed in terms of their possession of the skills or control of the techniques which enable the discharge of the jobs which keep the system going in conformity with the expectations of managerialist rationality (ibid., 9–26).

Clearly, this form of rationality is perfectly adapted to the animating concerns and workings of capitalism/empire, out of which in fact it seems to have issued. When moved into the world of education (as the description of Lankan ELT practice above indicates that it has been), therefore, it guarantees the vulnerability of that world to the teleological prescriptions of capitalism/empire. The modern world of education (within which the ELT world belongs) had, from the moment of its beginnings in its present form around the time of the Reformation and Renaissance in Europe, developed a base in response to those prescriptions, as administered by the emerging dominant politico-socioeconomic group, the middle class (see Graff 1987). Particularly as it moved into the nineteenth century and beyond, a lot of the kind of literacy it aimed to develop was 'functional to the industrial mode of production', directed significantly towards 'the reproduction of the labour force and of the relations of production' (Verne 1981, 291).

The appropriation of the Lankan ELT world by managerialist rationality, therefore, ensures its servitude to capitalism/empire. That this is so is confirmed by the fact that it began increasingly to manifest itself patently in that world with the commencement of the 'restoration' of English and the movement away from socialism and welfarism towards an 'open economy', which signalled the final acquiescence by the leadership in the structuring operations of global capitalism. Salleh (2000), writing when this movement had reached a kind of peak, makes the links impossible not to recognise. Censuring the education system then in place for its misguided preoccupation with 'equity', which had led only to unemployment (prominently so among a volatile, educated youth, who were, consequently, ready fuel for violent subversive activity), economic stagnation, and so on, Salleh suggests an alternative set of concerns, efficiency, effectiveness, quality and relevance, directed towards an effort to integrate the national economy with the global free economy. These concerns would be defined in highly instrumental terms, with reference to the extent to which the education system could increase the competitiveness of its products (many currently not just unemployed but 'unemployable') in the local and global job markets, by equipping them with the kinds of 'knowledge, skills and attributes' which 'the market demands'. The pursuit of these concerns entailed inevitably the removal of significant segments of the system from state control and support (which included free education) and opening them to the private sector (and its fee-levying mechanisms). In terms of curriculum, it involved heavy emphasis on English and IT. In education in general, the focus fell centrally on 'information' (intermittently—and expediently—renamed 'knowledge') and 'skills', which carried particular value for instrumental reasons.

With regard to English, these various matters not only drove its 'restoration', but also, in the specific world of ELT, reinforced and consolidated a preoccupation which it had in fact begun to show earlier too, namely the preoccupation with packages of skills, methods, techniques, activity routines, strategies, operational procedures, and other such, which might collectively be termed, for ease of reference, the 'machinery' of the field. Given what Feyerabend (1988) has reminded us of, namely, the propensity of such machinery to take on a validity of their own and even, as it were, take over the subject and thinking involved, the inevitable corollary was a kind of willing suspension of the intellect (and, also, intelligence)—a gradual devaluing of intellectual effort (often derisively dismissed by resort to what was for some unfathomable reason believed to be an irrevocably condemnatory term, 'theoretical'), the loss of a capacity to discriminate or judge, and a readiness not to look at the actualities of the demands made on the pedagogical task by the specificities of the context. Not surprisingly, language education itself came to be seen reductively, in bureaucratic (or technocratic) terms, and a strong belief developed in the sufficiency of administrative solutions to what were perceived to be the educational problems involved, even though they often displayed obliviousness of substantive qualitative issues of education. The UGC subcommittee decision to assign to the service sector of the field of English studies major responsibility for restructuring the whole field, including its academic sector, for instance, betrays a troubling unawareness of and disregard for the very nature of academic disciplinarity (and this from the UGC!). It is not irrelevant to note that throughout the several years of its existence, the chairpersons of the subcommittee have been zoologists, microbiologists, and academics in computer technology, anything but those who have a specialised understanding of English language and of language education and planning.

An added wrinkle grafted on within the material realities of the Lankan context to such inevitable consequences of the reign of 'machinery' relates to two matters remarked on earlier, the phenomenon of credentialism, and the impact on it of the opportunistic indulgence by the leadership in populism. The latter, a very important strategy for persuading people that they have got from the unsound and contradictory measures advocated and pursued much more than in fact they have, issued with regard to credentialism as a readiness to issue paper qualifications at the end of rapidly proliferating new courses and programmes which, though they assisted in the career advancement of the holders, provided no guarantee that these holders had the expertise and skills to which they formally attested, let alone knowledge and understanding. Combined with the de-intellectualisation and bureaucratic philistinisation of the field, this has led to a massive mediocratisation of it (particularly at its higher levels), an incapacity among too many of the significant people who are involved to think the educational and pedagogical problems out with critical awareness and understanding of the fundamental qualitative issues involved and sensitivity to the nature of challenges raised by the complex specificities of the context.

The obvious consequence is the reduction of the local ELT world to a dependency of the global ELT industry and its agents. It is a dependency that is made up of a set of disenfranchised clients of the industry and its agents, who (passively receiving packages of 'stuff' from those who do the 'thinking' out there) apply them as prescribed, at best as skilled mechanics of the trade. In this they are supported by agencies of the industry that are themselves not particularly renowned for their transcendence of mediocrity, and, very notably, by the local comprador complicit in the whole operation. If anything, this is most obviously a re-enactment of the classic imperialist syndrome.

Interestingly, it seems to be very much this syndrome that the other matter dealt with in critiquing planning scholarship earlier, relating to the language problems of 'developing nations', also reflects. The large inadequacy of the confident pronouncements made on the challenges facing these nations is demonstrated particularly sharply by the descriptive and explanatory helplessness of the static taxonomising methodology of the schema. A scrutiny, against the background of the comments made above about material realities and coordinates, of the criteria used in setting up the taxonomy will indicate what the source of the failure is. All of them, directly associated with globalisation and involving modernisation, development and technology, reflect the priorities of capitalism/empire, which get valorised within the schema by its frequent references to a 'western language', the 'western counterparts' of the people in these countries, who are unquestioningly assumed to define a kind of desirable goal for the latter to set their sights by, and so on.

In these respects, the planning scholarship of the time reflected the deportment of the 'development decades' (as they have been termed) within which it was developing. During those decades, the developed countries of Euro-America were assumed to define the 'centre', by reference to which the 'underdeveloped' countries were measured as lacking, constituted as the 'other', and consigned to the insignificant peripheries (Kandiah 2001a). Such assumptions were central to the epistemological subversion and appropriation of these countries, a task which could no longer be addressed in the former taken-for-granted ways now that the countries had received independence and were not colonies in the material sense. The schema under critique may, on the basis of its characterisation above, be considered to be pursuing just this same epistemological project, but in the specialised field of language planning. Its failures of description and explanation may then be seen not only to reflect its metatheoretical inadequacies in the face of the complexities of the material realities of these countries, but also to call attention to other deleterious features of it, relating to matters of ideology, politics, power and hegemony, all of which naturally bring up issues of ethics too.

Interestingly, the discussion of the other large planning matter addressed in this paper, relating to ELT pedagogy, also followed the same polemical curve, moving from what was claimed to be a necessary engagement with the material coordinates of the activity under consideration to an identification, on that basis, of the metatheoretical shortcomings involved, and from there to a clarification of issues of ideology, politics, and so on, which pointed directly to salient issues of ethics and the failure of rational communication and interaction among the groups involved.

To the extent that the argumentation carries conviction, it would provide support to the basic claims made in the paper. The hope is that in doing so, it might indicate how language and language-education planning scholarship might move towards more satisfactory levels of descriptive and explanatory (perhaps even observational) adequacy than at present; and, further, that on that basis it might also contribute, to the development of both the more effective and the more ethical praxis that can make a positive difference to the human subjects who ultimately lie at the heart of both the scholarship and the activity it studies.

References

Ahmad, A. 1992. *In Theory: Classes, Nations, Literatures*. London: Verso.

Fanon, F. 1968. *The Wretched of the Earth*. New York: Grove Press.

Feyerabend, P. 1988. *Against Method*. Rev. ed. London: Verso.

Graff, H.J. 1987. *The Legacies of Literacy: Continuities and Contradictions in Western Culture and Society*. Bloomington: Indiana University Press.

Jiggins, J. 1979. *Caste and Politics in the Politics of the Sinhalese 1947– 1976*. London: Cambridge University Press.

Kandiah, T. 1984. *Kaduva*: Power and the English Language Weapon in Sri Lanka. In *Honouring E.F.C. Ludowyk,* eds. P. Colin-Thomé and A.Halpé. Colombo: Tisara Prakasakayo.

————————. 1995. Centering the Periphery of English: Towards Participatory Communities of Discourse. Foreword to *Parakrama*. xv-xxxvii.

————————. 2000. Re-visioning, Revolution, Revisionism: English and the Ambiguities of Post-colonial Practice. *The Sri Lanka Journal of the Humanities,* 24 & 25 (1998–1999). 31–64.

————————. 2001. Whose Meanings? Probing the Dialectics of English as a Global Language. In *Ariels – Departures and Returns: Essays for Edwin Thumboo*, eds. C.K. Tong et al. Singapore: Oxford University Press.

————————. 2003. De-/Re-centering Thought and Practice in Third World English Language Studies: From the Materiality of the Word to the Determinate Materiality of Time and Place. In *Critical Discourse Analysis: The*

Message of the Medium (A New Intellectual Perspective for English Studies in Yemen), ed. C.N. Srinivasan. Yemen: Hodeidah University.

————. 2004. The Challenge of Developing a Viable Modern Academic Tradition of Post-colonial Language Scholarship: A Sri Lankan Contextualisation. In *The Yearbook of South Asian Languages and Linguistics,* ed. Rajendra Singh. Berlin: Mouton.

Marshall, D. 1986. Rebuttal Essay. *International Journal of the Sociology of Language*. 60: 201–211.

Matterlart, A. 1983. Introduction: For a Class and Group Analysis of Popular Communication Practices. In *Communication and the Caste Struggle, Volume 2: Liberation, Socialism*, eds. A. Matterlart and S. Siegelaub New York: International General.

Salleh, F. 2002. Education: What is the Right Model for Sri Lanka? *Daily Mirror*, May 2, 2002.

Siegelaub, S. 1983. Preface: Working Notes on Social Relations in Communication and Culture. In A. Matterlart and S. Sieglaub, eds. 11–16.

Verne, E. 1981. Literacy and Industrialisation – The Dispossession of Speech. In *Literacy and Social Development in the West: A Reader,* ed. H.G. Graff. Bloomington: Indiana University Press.

Yeatman, A. 1990. *Bureaucrats, Technocrats, Femocrats: Essays on the Contemporary Australian State*. Sydney: Allen and Unwin.

4

Patterns of Bilingualism in the New World Order: The South Asian Scene

K. Chellappan

Bilingualism and multilingualism flourished even in ancient and medieval societies, the Tower of Babel being probably the prototype, though with negative connotations. In medieval Europe, Latin was the cultural lingua franca of Europe, where each nation had its own local languages. In India, Sanskrit was the cultural lingua franca along with other regional languages, and there was interaction between Sanskrit and other languages as well as among the regional languages themselves. Even with the rise of the nation state, the 'one-language, one-nation theory' did not work. With the advent of colonialism, though the coloniser's language tried to dominate, there were other voices, often heard only at the lower, but the deeper level. In the postcolonial and postindustrial era again we see a new kind of bilingualism as globalisation and localisation are taking place simultaneously everywhere (Fishman 1998).

While English has emerged as a global and glocal language, other languages have also made their legitimate claims in the new world order. Bilingualism or even multilingualism has become the order of the day and has contributed to the dialogic interaction between and within nations and individuals, and to the creation of a heterogeneous humanity in a world without walls.

In most countries, local languages have become emblems of cultural identity as well as the means of constructing a new nationality. As During (1995, 125–126) says, 'in both literature and politics, the postcolonial drive towards identity centres around language, partly because in postmodernity, identity is barely available elsewhere. For the postcolonial to speak or write in the imperial tongues is to call forth a problem of identity, to be thrown into mimicry and ambivalence. The question of language for postcolonialism is political, cultural and literary as 'in the material sense a choice of language is a choice of identity'. The former colonies have retained English as a medium of intranational and international communication. The spread of English today is a consequence of colonisation, and it is a contributor to globalisation. In the process, the language has become a global language. However, its use is confined to certain purposes and certain classes.

Fishman (1998, 28–29) has rightly said that 'the brief formal educational contact that most learners have with English is too scant to produce lasting literacy, fluency or even comprehension. Indeed, for all the enthusiasm and vitriol generated by grand-scale globalisation, it is the growth in regional interactions—trade, travel, the spread of religions, interethnic marriages—that touches the widest array of local populations. These interactions promote the spread of regional languages'. For example, in West Africa, Hausa is not only the native language of more than 25 million people, but it is also a second or third language for more than double the number, and serves as the language of commerce and regional contacts. Swahili enjoys a similar position in East Africa. In China, Mandarin Chinese is the most dominant link language though English also has entered the outer fringe. Spanish, French and pidgin English are spreading along with the native languages in America, the former French colonies and Australia respectively. This indicates that along with English, there are other languages fulfilling various functions in different regions.

As lmtiaz Hasnain (1997, 72) says, 'one of the characteristics of South Asian bilingualism is that despite prolonged contact, monolingual situation still remains the norm'. Applying the neoclassical model of economic theory, Hasnain arrives at a tripartite distinction to describe the time allocated by bilinguals to majority language and minority language activities: 'If the practice of an activity increases by a greater percentage than income, it is considered "superior"; if the practice of an activity decreases although income increases, the activity in question is "inferior." "Normal" are those activities whose practice does not increase in proportion to income' (ibid., 72).

South Asian countries share a common ethos as well as history, and their ethos is characterised by coexistence of which language is the main vehicle and symbol. Sanskrit, Prakrit, Urdu and Tamil constituted the linguistic core of this region in the premodern era, and we now see South Asia as a virtual linguistic museum—with conflicting local languages and English assuming the role of the arbitrator. However, as nations often define themselves through languages, they become both a source of integration and division even in South Asia. If the creation of Pakistan was based on a religious principle, the formation of Bangladesh was shaped by linguistic factors. To give another illustration, in Sri Lanka the ethnic problem was fuelled by language and, to some extent, by religion. There has, thus, always been a nexus between language, religion and ethnicity.

To take the case of India, the idea of unifying the country through a national language did not work. In fact, the concept of one national language itself was in conflict with national unity. The idea of linguistic demarcation of states was meant to educate the masses through their own language and give the people of each state a cultural identity. King (1987) shows how the drive for linguistic states was also impelled by aspirations grounded in communal rivalries among groups grappling for power. Language coalesces and conflicts with a number of other factors, and the very means of utility and identity has become a source of division and disruption. This is not only because of the power within the language, but also because of that behind the language.

Along with a kind of horizontal bilingualism with reference to the local or regional languages there is also vertical bilingualism: English vis-à-vis the local/regional language. Whereas Crystal (1997) claims that there is a South Asian variety of English, Kachru (1998,91) refers to English as an Asian language: 'English in one way or another, has indeed a presence in the most vital aspects of Asian lives—our cultures, our languages, our interactional patterns, our discourse, our economies and indeed, in our politics. But, above all, in transforming our identities, as individuals and societies, and the identities of our languages. These transformations are evident in a variety of contact languages and literatures, both in Asia and other parts of the world'.

According to Crystal (1997, 43) 'English has, as a consequence, retained its standing within Indian society, continuing to be used within the legal system, government administration, secondary and higher education, the armed forces, the media, business, and tourism. It is a strong unifying force. In the Dravidian-speaking areas of the south, it is widely preferred to Hindi as a lingua franca. In the north, its fortunes vary from state to state, in relation to Hindi depending on the policies of those in power. In Pakistan, it is an associate official language. It has no official status in the other countries of South Asia, but throughout the region it is universally used as the medium of international communication' (1997, 43).

Both statements require qualification. It is true that English is still used in administration, law, education and media, but it holds only an associate position with the national languages. Hence, there is a kind of bilingual transaction in most of these areas. In all these cases, the larger chunk of the society uses only the local languages.

Again, it is true that English has acquired a regional identity—by absorbing the local cultures and acquiring linguistic features common to this region. Crystal (ibid., 133) claims that 'there is one group in India, Pakistan, Bangladesh and Sri Lanka, often collectively called South Asian English'. This, however, does not mean that this variety of English can express the deeper levels of our culture and consciousness. As Wa Thiong'o (1986, 28) remarks, 'Language as culture is the collective memory bank of a people's experience in history.'

Even Indian English writers like Rushdie (1983, 28) feel their estrangement from their history while using English, and though the writer's English is becoming more and more British in idiom and style, he feels that he cannot sever his connections with the East: 'It is part of the world to which, whether I like it or not, I am still joined, if only by elastic bands.' However, both his heroes Khayam and Saleem fear being alienated from and by history. In writers like A.K. Ramanujan and Kamala Das, there is a kind of bilingual– trilingual synthesis. Whereas Ramanujan says that he spoke Kannada in the kitchen, Tamil in the playground, but wrote in English, Kamala Das says that she dreams in one language and writes in another. Yasmine Gooneratne demonstrates the dialogic nature of boundary crossing at the transnational level in her poem 'At the barrier'.

> This way, the neon lights say, and Have your papers ready.
> "Your passport, please. A student. Did you have
> a pleasant stay? Anything to declare?" No accent, scent or spirits
>
> exceeding regulations. "Anything
> declared here on your outward journey and
> not brought back?" A religion
> mislaid one morning in an empty church
> and never found again. A few ideals
> locally made; that don't pass current there
> but have some value for me. Here they are.
> "Anything bought in Britain upon which
> you should pay duty?" A liking for this place.
> I hope they'll let me keep it?

Though most of the Indian English writers try to appropriate and acculturate English by giving it a specific identity and thereby reveal their own identity, English cannot claim to be the best medium for discovering our roots and dreaming our dreams. However, English serves to reflect one kind of identity by its absorption of certain strata of our history and culture. This has to coexist with the role of our Asian languages, which have also felt the impact of English. What is more important though is the need to bring together the Asian languages, and English does have a useful role to play in this process.

From the point of view of knowledge dissemination, English is said to be the source of information in science and technology. It does not mean our Asian languages cannot be developed or used for this purpose. In fact, the roots of cognition and creativity embedded in the mother tongue must be tapped for learning science and technology. A policy of interpenetration of languages for mutual benefit must inform the pedagogy and percolate the classroom. Whereas South Asian languages can express culture and fulfil certain cognitive functions, South Asian English can be used for commerce and science.

All this points to the need for simultaneous convergence and divergence of languages in use at the level of the individual, state, nation and region. We can bring about convergence among various Asian languages through multilingual dictionaries and translations with English and/ or Sanskrit/ Urdu/ Tamil as link languages. The Regional Institute of English's (RIE's) project on a dictionary of Dravidian languages, with English equivalents, is a case in point. We can have similar projects for northern languages, with Sanskrit and English equivalents. In Sri Lanka we can have a similar project with Sinhalese, Tamil, Sanskrit and English. We can expand this pattern for Pakistan and Bangladesh, taking into account Urdu. Thus, South Asian languages can meet at several points, and English will be a good companion to all of them. An institute for SAARC languages should be established to study the links and evolve strategies for developing and teaching them together.

This will help us forge a South Asian identity and unity in terms of culture through our Asian languages as well as English, and intraregional and international communication and trade through English as well as the regional languages. Ultimately, identity and unity can coexist like languages do, and the very walls which divided them can become windows into our neighbours' homes as well as the world. In fact, one of our new commandments should be: 'Love thy neighbour's tongue as thy own.' A healthy bilingual approach to our own languages as well as English can help us forge a South Asian unity and identity irrespective of ethnic, linguistic, political and religious diversity, and this unity is more a recovery than a discovery.

References

Crystal, D. 1997. *English as a Global Language*. Cambridge: Cambridge University Press.

During, S. 1995. Postmodernism or Post-colonialism Today? In *The Post-colonial Studies Reader*, eds. B. Ashcroft, G. Griffith and H. Tiffin. London: Routledge.

Fishman, J. 1998. The New Linguistic Order. *Foreign Policy*. Winter 1998/99. 26–39.

Hasnain, I. 1997. New Economic Policy and the Fate of Minor Languages. In *Translation and Multiculturalism*, ed. Santha Ramakrishna. Delhi: Pencraft.

Kachru, B. 1998. English as an Asian Language, *Links and Letters 5:* 89–108.

King, R.D. 1987. *Nehru and the Language Politics of India*. London: Oxford University Press.

Rushdie, S. 1983. *Shame*. London: Jonathan Cape.

Wa Thiong'o, N. 1986. *Decolonising the Mind: The Politics of Language in African Literature*. London : James Curry.

5

English and Globalisation: Language Management in Cross-Cultural Settings

Lachman M. Khubchandani

The multilingual world, armed with new communication technologies, has created a new situation of haves and have-nots in a digital divide. It is, therefore, necessary to give clear expression not only to the rights of individuals and speech communities that belong to smaller languages, but also to the duties of all the agencies concerned (including dominant language groups such as those advocating global English) and the obligations of the state and international forums.

Most of the regions in South Asia are marked by plurality of cultures and languages in one space village, town, district, state— and nation. India is a case in point. The country has been a laboratory of plurilingual ethos down the ages. In this milieu, an organic complementation of different languages has thrived through various processes of synergy that include putting forth one's efforts, and serendipity, or accepting the other on his/her own terms and being open to fusion in language use.

This paper discusses a few issues of language management in cross-cultural settings, as demonstrated in plurilingual India, in the light of the recent thrust on Information Communication Technology (ICT). It highlights the problems of cross-cultural conceptual systems when linking the reality through the metaphors of a non-native language such as English.

The postcolonial situation

There has been a growing acceptance of English by many corporate bodies spread over the former British colonies in spheres such as education, technology, journalism and creative writing as a medium of 'superlayered' sensibility. English tradition in South Asia, as a whole, is marked by the strength of two non-native traditions: a double bind of the colonial past and of communication technology, discussed in detail elsewhere (Khubchandani 1997). Cultural forces of colonial domination still continue to haunt the language scene through the power exercised by the westernised elite in language development programmes.

Postcolonial developments in language use in many newly independent countries are characterised by power struggles where the control has shifted from outside colonisers to the creamy layer of their societies: the 'white man' is replaced by the 'brown saheb' as is glaringly evident in the contemporary South Asian context. Tussles on the language front between the established elite in these countries, pressurising for status quo (explicitly or implicitly), and assertions of the emerging elite for cultural and national resurgence through local (dominant/minority) languages bring out this dilemma eloquently. Many complex social and political agendas influence the choice of the medium of education in different parts of the globe (UNESCO 2003, Khubchandani 2005).

The adoption of the colonial language English as a 'transitory', neutral lingua franca by many developing countries is viewed as a kind of linguistic imperialism (Phillipson 1992). The entry and sustenance of English in the non-native world on such a massive scale reveals the extent to which a language could be adapted to meet new challenges. A few studies of English in the non-native world point to the extent colonial English has penetrated different walks of life, highlighting the economic and political pressures which assign it a global status for cross-cultural purposes (Crystal 1997, Pennycook 1998, Fishman1998, Tollefson and Tsui 2004). There have been studies of the Indian reality too (Agnihotri and Khanna 1993, Kachru 1982, 1983, Khubchandani 1983, 1996, Schiffman 1996).

Today English has acquired an aura of the unparalleled universal language on the politico-economic, technological and academic scene. On the political scene, there has been an intense debate during the past five decades about reallocating the role of English in India. In the midst of conflicting solutions at the ideological level, policies of the union and state governments, no doubt, lay stress on shedding the dominance of imperial English and on assigning new roles to indigenous languages in public life.

But at the same time, at the societal level, English has continued to be an important part of the communication matrix in urban India (and is getting rapidly extended to rural India). There has been a glaring proliferation of English seeping through the upper crust of the society to the middle class, and further down to the grassroots level, particularly in the urban settings (Khubchandani 1983). In this context, one should take note of the rapidly growing phenomenon characterised as 'passive smoking' of English in the urban milieu where individuals can passively 'get by' with the rudiments of English without having systematically learnt the language in school.

Imperial English, as a tool of the social elite in India seems to encourage an obsession with western values, which are often censored in political debates as the 'brown saheb mentality'. Such issues raise serious questions about the vitality of a non-native language on a foreign soil: Can English in India acquire indigenous vigour like any other Indian language? Are the thinking processes in a plural society insulated within the bounds of a particular language or do they transcend across languages over a wider spectrum, native as well as second and third languages, available to plurilingual societies? Does India's present education system facilitate the thinking of its people in its 'own' national languages, or does it perpetuate the nation's dependency on imperial English? These questions raise serious doubts over the emphasis being laid on distinguishing the authenticity of native versus non-native nuances of English.

Non-native Englishes

A native speaker inherits the language conventions in a holistic manner; but she/he cannot claim monopoly over its conventions when it acquires the role of a contact or a liaison language. On the other hand, acquisition of non-native speech is primarily guided by the dictates of relevance.[1] A non-native speaker has a brush with merely a few domains of the second language in complementation with his native language, and it does not commit him to the native tradition in its entirety.[2]

During the colonial rule, imperial powers generally treated non-native speakers of a language as 'marginal' in shaping the norms of the second language they acquired. Ideal expectations were that a non-native speaker should faithfully toe the line of the target language's native tradition by submitting to the dictates of its custodians and standardising agencies.[3]

Such diverse perceptions lead us to understand the non-native phenomenon of a language in a broader perspective. It is necessary to identify a crucial distinction between the communication rights of native speakers and those of instrumental non-native users of a particular language. Language communicates experience and, in this process, a contact language like English in the Indian plural setting has gradually been transcending the bounds of the culture of its origin.

English, on the one hand, is getting further detached from native English (British or American) models; and on the other, with the

---

[1]China is a case in point. In the mid-seventies, an American delegation of linguists visited China (it included Charles Ferguson, William Labov and others). One visitor enquired of the interpreter about the reasons for the popularity of learning English in the country. The interpreter pointed out in a matter-of-factmanner that the learning of English had become very popular in China as 'We are keen to propagate the thoughts of Mao Tse Tung through English to the rest of the world.' This may be a blunt admission of the instrumentalist viewpoint of learning a foreign language (Khubchandani 2003).

[2]With reference to the dialectics in the studies on chaos (Gleick 1987, 309), an apt analogy will be that of contrasting the difference between the solidifying of water in an ice-tray from outside to inside (similar to the bounds of a tradition) and the transforming of water molecules (i.e., crystallising, melting and re-crystallising) into snowflakes (similar to the acquisition of a second language). It is called the lightning-rod effect, 'a delicate balance between forces of stability and forces of instability; a powerful interplay of forces on atomic scales and forces on everyday scales' (for a detailed discussion, see Khubchandani 1996).

[3]Enoch Powell's remarks in the British Parliament in 1988 endorse this view: 'Others may speak or read English more or less—but it is our language, not theirs. It was made in England by the English and it remains our distinctive property, however widely it is learnt or used.' (quoted in Greenbaum 1990, 15)

pulls of modernisation the scope and the intensity of communication in English have been rapidly increasing. Many people in India, obsessed with the colonial past, exhibit an impeccable command, a native-like grasp, over imperial English. But on the other hand, there are many workers, including domestic help, who speak English merely as a means of earning a livelihood (Khubchandani and Hosali 1997).

The metamorphosis in the non-native speech creates a distinct profile on the 'alien' soil (or in international forums) which may or may not be intimately connected to the native model. The vitality of grassroots English in India reveals innovation and creativity in reduplication, collocation and imagery. All these developments take Indian English, as a complementary code, to a divergent path quite remote from native models of English. A few language surveys, conducted in recent years, capture the phenomenon of linguistic variation in a variety of Englishes (from grassroots to near-native) in use in the Indian subcontinent. A new supplement added to the recent edition of the Oxford English Dictionary, authenticating over 3,300 Indianisms in standard English, has brought a sense of jubilation among many anglophiles in India—indeed a postcolonial trait of 'works and forms created here but evaluated there'!

The domineering impact of globalisation through the upsurge of ICT has created imbalances: the encroaching 'exploitative' communication networks are regarded as attributes of powerful 'strong' languages (such as imperial English), and 'accommodating' complementary communication networks of minority languages are evaluated as powerless 'weak' languages. Many developing nations are caught in resolving the tensions of the local versus the global; there could be varied local responses to the fast pace of globalisation. It may produce nationals who are ambivalent about their own identity and nations stripped of their rich cultural heritage (Khubchandani 1995). Probal Dasgupta (2004) refers to this overshadowing phenomenon of English in the Indian context as a 'hijacking attribute' of global English, whereby Indian languages are held at ransom.

The Indian urban landscape in a plurilingual milieu highlights the dominant use of local Englishes in the print media, television networks, and advertising on public displays. A preliminary study, based on the data obtained from these networks gives positive evidence in favour of Indian *angrezi* acquiring the vigour and vitality to represent urban reality. Such traits lead to the internalisation of English, manifested through (a) a linguistic projection of indigenous environment and of non-native sensibility, (b) a language of cerebration revealed through frequent code-switching (such as in advertising), and (c) a vehicle of creative expression, or innovating new nuances through the use of English (in literary as well as nonliterary domains). Indo-Anglian expression draws its vitality from cross-cultural fertilisations.

Cross-cultural conceptual systems

In cross-cultural settings, configurations of traditional and industrial milieus are bound to affect one another. In a climate of mutual trust and respect, this contact encourages a positive blend through synergy and serendipity, as discussed earlier. On the other hand, when the norms and values of one culture dominate the other (such as those emerging from the colonial experience), these tend to generate dissonance between the two, or result in the assimilation of the weaker culture (in demographic or economic terms) with the dominating one (Khubchandani 1990). Here a distinction is made between 'internationalisation' (or a transnational networking of communications), similar to McLuhan's global village, as poignantly depicted in the Sanskrit dictum *vasudhaiva kutumbakam,* or 'All the universe is a family.'

Every culture possesses a certain ritualistic chord of personal interaction cultivated through the long history of its social life. These factors have a significant bearing in the processes of decision-making, implementation and coordination. In everyday transactions one understands or experiences reality through metaphors, by drawing upon associations in a coherent manner from one's cultural, intellectual and rhetorical traditions (Lakoff and Johnson 1980). It is, in a way, a metaphorical device of 'relating one kind of thing in terms of another'. The language user internalises these metaphorical concepts unique to his/her tradition. To understand a conceptual scheme through its metaphorical links is an empirical science, an anthropological exercise, which is not necessarily bound by any rational paradigm.

The conceptualisation of reality through the metaphorical links of a non-native language such as English can pose certain problems. Viewing the issue from an Indian background, it will be relevant to reflect on values associated with English terms such as 'work', 'action' and 'activity'. In everyday discourse, the term 'work' implies an apparent activity; it is related to an observable product with apparent benefits (mostly socioeconomic). In contrast, the Sanskrit term *karman* (Hindi *kaam*)—based on the Sanskrit root *kr.* 'to do, to make', and its extensions *kartaa* (maker), *krta* (deed, completed task), *kriyaa* (making, doing)—carries with it quite a different series of expectations. In this regard, a project at the University of California examined in detail the notion of *karma* in Indian thought (Keyes and Daniel 1983). The term *karman* can be referred to as 'a thing made/done' in English; it incorporates all acts, including many mental activities. According to the Sanskrit conceptual system, every activity, apparent or not so apparent, is considered to be *kriyaa* 'making' (Vatsyayana 1939). In English, thinking compassionate thoughts or faithfully thinking of God are not regarded as spontaneous 'doings'. In Sanskrit 'seeing', 'hearing' are regularly counted as mental acts, whereas in English, one does not need to *act* to hear a noise.

In the metaphysical context, the theory of *karma* has emerged from the domain of 'mental acts'. *Karman* is extended to *samskaar* (traces) where something is made, someone is benefited, and some purpose leads the activity to a series of constructs to satisfy expectations; the body is retained beyond one's birth for the *bhoga* (experience) of *sukha/dukha* (satisfying or frustrating experience). In the light of this, the term *nishkaam karma*, outside the paradigm of *dharma, varna,* and *punarjanma* (rebirth), can be distorted in literal translation as 'selfless act' or 'an act done without expecting any fruit'.

There are problems of indeterminacy in translating from one culture into another which can lead to ethnocentric, parochial interpretations. It will, therefore, be more rewarding if in a scientific discourse, when debating conceptual systems across cultures, the total connotation of a term is explicated by retaining it in the original along with its metaphors, which are shared by its native speakers (Nair 2002).

Gandhiji realised the vitality of culture-bound concepts when communicating with the Indian masses and brought into currency terms from the Indian reality, such as *swadeshi, satyaagrah, ahimsaa, harijan* and *raamraajya*. In a scientific discourse such cross-cultural distortions become more transparent. For example, *dharma* is narrowly interpreted as 'religion', and *jaati, varna* and *gotra* are bracketed under the term 'caste'. Similarly, the concept of 'secularism' is beyond the reach of an average Indian mind, and its translations in Indian languages are not very satisfactory. The Sanskrit coinage *dharma nirpekshataa,* or 'religious neutrality', appears to be a hollow term; a metaphor like *vasudhaiva kutumbakam*, cited earlier, will be better understood in the context of Indian reality. Due to the overwhelming political and economic pressures in the pursuit of development, limitations of this kind at the cognitive level have not yet been fully realised by the Indian academia.

Conclusion

The Indian experience demonstrates that an understanding of plural societies will largely be guided by viewing language as a synergic network inspiring mutual trust in cross-cultural settings. For a successful transplantation of English as an effective complementary tool of communication and comprehension in a plural society like India, it will be necessary to probe into varied roles played by the English-speaking elite in lending a constructive hand to develop Indian languages. From the demographic viewpoint, India—representing nearly one-sixth of humanity—can have a significant impact on the future course of globalisation. To what extent can the legislative, judicial and executive wings of the state help in diffusing the politicisation of language development?

It is time to set aside the rhetoric of retaining or banishing 'colonial' English in toto and work out strategies of developing a multilingual milieu relevant to our needs in the changed situation. There should be mutual trust between the English elite and the masses in the process of nation building. In the next few decades it will be interesting to watch the developments concerning the content and functions of the *angrezi* lingua franca among non-native speech groups and their interface with the native English world.

References

Agnihotri R.K. and L. Khanna, eds. 1993. *Second Language Acquisition: Socio-Cultural Aspects of English in India*. New Delhi: Sage Publications.

Crystal, D. 1997. *English as a Global Language*. Cambridge: Cambridge University Press.

Dasgupta, P. 2004. India's Languages Tomorrow: Three Scenarios. In *Language, Society and Culture: ZICR: Visitations to 21st Century Realities*, eds. U.N. Singh, N.H. Itagi and S.K. Singh. Mysore: Central Institute of Indian Languages.

Fishman, J.A. 1998. The New Linguistic Order, *Foreign Policy*, Winter. Washington. 26–40; reprint 2000. In *Globalization and the Challenges of a New Century*, eds. P. O' Meara, et al. Bloomington: Indiana University Press.

Gleick, J. 1987. *Chaos : Making a New Science.* London: Cardinal.

Greenbaum, S. 1990. "Whose English?" In *The State of the Language*, eds. C. Ricks and L Michaels. London: Faber & Faber.

Kachru, B.B., ed. 1982. *The Other Tongue: English Across Cultures*. Urbana: University of Illinois Press.

———. 1983. *The Indianization of English: The English Language in India*. New Delhi: Oxford University Press.

Keyes, C.F. and L. Daniel. 1983. *Karma: An Anthropological Inquiry*. Berkeley: University of California Press.

Khubchandani, L. 1983. *Plural Languages, Plural Cultures: Communication, Identity and Sociopolitical Change in Contemporary India*. Honolulu: University of Hawaii Press, East-West Center Book.

———. 1990. Concept of Work Across Cultures. In *The Concept Work in Indian Society*, ed. A.D. Moddie. Shimla: Indian Institute of Advanced Study.

———. 1995. Universal and Unique in Cross-cultural Interaction: A Paradigm Shift in Development Ideology. In *Interface of Cultural Identity and Development. Proceedings of UNESCO Experts Meet on Culture and Development*, ed. B.N. Saraswati. New Delhi: Indira Gandhi National Centre of Arts.

———. 1996. English Snowflakes in Indian Tropics. *South Asian Language Review* VI: 1:84–93. New Delhi.

———. 1997. *Revisualizing Boundaries: A Plurilingual Ethos*. New Delhi: Sage Publications.

———. 2003. Language Harmony and Language Collisions : Dynamics of Diversity at the Grassroots. In *When Languages Collide: Perspectives on Language Conflict, Language Competition, and Language Coexistence*, eds. B.D. Joseph, et al. Columbus: The Ohio State University Press.

———. 2005. Medium of Instruction: Interplay of Politics and Pedagogy. Review of 2004. eds. J W. Tollefson and A.B.M. Tsui, forthcoming.

Khubchandani, L.M. and P. Hosali. 1997. Grassroots English in a Communication Paradigm. South Asian Language Association Round Table Conference. New Delhi: Jawaharlal Nehru University; also published 1999 in *Language Problems and Language Planning* 23.3. Amsterdam: John Benjamins. pp. 251–72.

Lakoff, G. and M. Johnson. 1980. *Metaphors We Live By*. Chicago: University of Chicago Press.

McLuhan, M. and B.B. Powers. 1989. *The Global Village: Transformations in World Life and Media in the 21st Century*. New York: Oxford University Press.

Nair, Rukmini Bhaya. 2002. *Translation, Trust and Theory: A Paradigm of India*. New Delhi: Sage Publication.

Pennycook, A. 1998. *English and the Discourses of Colonialism*. London: Routledge.

Phillipson, R., 1992. *Linguistic Imperialism*. Oxford: Oxford University Press.

Tollefson, J.W. and Amie B.M. Tsui, eds. 2004. *Medium of Instruction Policies: Which Agenda? Whose Agenda*? Mahwah, N J: Lawrence Erlbaum.

UNESCO. 2003. Education in a Multilingual World. An Education Position Paper. Paris.

Vatsyayana. 1939. *Nyayabhasya*. Trans. Ganganath Jha, Poona Oriental Series 59. Pune: Deccan College Postgraduate Research Institute.

6

Sustainable Scenarios in Indian Language Cultivation

Probal Dasgupta

The industrial hijack of language

The present paper considers in some detail the form of the presence of English in India. The argument here is that this presence and, by extension, the presence of English in many other societies represents an industrial hijack of the cognitive. Recognising this and taking appropriate action is a prerequisite for any recovery of cognitive health in and outside India. By this I do not wish to imply that the facts are the same throughout South Asia. Language policy in Bangladesh, Sri Lanka and Nepal, for instance, has given English a foreign rather than second language status, which possibly changes the affective map very slightly compared to India. But in those societies as well, the intellectual centre of gravity has been permitted to shift to English, with very similar consequences.

The speakers of Indian languages have mortgaged the cognitive sector of their verbality to the techno-industrial leviathan whose antics I cannot describe here in adequate concreteness. For my present purposes, I will call it just 'the industrial'. In India, the industrial take-over of our cognitive functions takes the form of a certain English monopolising all discursive and analytical enunciation work and leaving the expressive sector to the Indian languages. The Indian elite that has grown up under this monopoly has a certain English identity. This is not to deny that many members of this elite lead their personal lives in Indian languages and conduct only specified types of business in English. The point is that the national elite as a whole has an investment in that language as a definer of the functioning and reproduction of the entire elite. This investment has led to the emergence of an English-focused, expressive subcommunity of virtually monoglot Indians. Call it the anglophone elite. Its existence may be read as a marker of the broader national elite's commitment to the more than auxiliary use of English, of that elite's commitment to a partial identity-marking role for English in India.

Had this commitment been total or on the verge of becoming so, we would have expected to see signs of languages such as Marathi, Bangla, Telugu and Kannada, losing their hold over their respective constituencies. Then we would have little to discuss. But that is not the scene. Hence, my image of a hijack rather than a killing.

That the scene is complex becomes especially clear when we look at the split lexis of modern Indian languages and at the extreme underdevelopment of the audio-visual expressive industry in India's English-speaking sector. To unpack the first point, in any typical modern Indian language, all speakers agree in using a generous sprinkling of unassimilated English words representing categories such as technicality or the world of remunerative labour. And yet, in the same language, all writers agree in systematically replacing these words with a whole battery of variably stable neologisms coined during various waves of the native term-production enterprise. This is the split-lexis fact about this country's modern languages. When they wax technical, they speak English but they write translationese. Now to unpack our second point: the numerous anglophone Indians see fit to adapt themselves to the entertainment habits of two distinct populations—the Indian language population, which patronises the films, the popular songs, and other subjectivity-stroking industries in Indian languages; and the global anglophone population, which forms a massive outer market for Anglo-American media products. Despite the means, motive and opportunity, there is no Indian popular culture in English to offer an arena of light, unconscious and, therefore, collective self-articulation for this country's English-focused subcommunity. There is some NRI production in this domain, but its numerically limited reception in India and the fact that there is no indigenous Indian production of the same sort means that this basic fact about the economy is robust.

Those were the points. Firstly, the split lexis, shows that speakers of Indian languages regard the English usurpation of their cognitive sector as a temporary arrangement, not to be welcomed into serious Indian language use. This shows that it is a hijack. Secondly, the extreme underdevelopment of the anglophone-Indian popular-culture industry, indicates that not just the apparent victims, but even the apparent agents of the hijack take it to be a provisional state of affairs that one is shacking up in, not a cultural home that one can inhabit as an incipient community of English-speaking Indians who construct or vicariously sponsor a collective self-expression system.

These and related facts, reviewed elsewhere, seem to support the idea that a person looking for identities in this country will find expressively articulated and tradition-bearing identities only in the Indian languages, and that, if you need identity to be a community, then there is no such thing as a community of anglophone Indians held together by their common language. There is arguably a coherent set of potential migrants to anglophone countries, and those who have already migrated have kin groups in India, but these do not function as an anglophone Indian ethnicity resident in India. I will employ the term anglophone Indians to designate certain individuals, and I will speak of them as a community the way one speaks of 'the academic community', without assuming that anglophone Indians have an ethnic identity as such a community. What is an open question is whether such a community is anthropologically real. On the face of it, it is not.

However, this reasonable first reading of the facts rests on an uncritical acceptance of the naïve dichotomy between the cognitive sector of language use, hijacked in this country by the industrial language English and the expressive sector, which such a division of cultural labour reserves for the Indian languages, appearing to explain the lack of a popular cultural base in English. What if we question the neatness of the cognitive vs expressive dichotomy?

The details of the literary basis of the NRI writing take-off that took place in the eighties and became evident in the nineties lend themselves to the task of posing what look like the right questions. It transpires that a knowledge-inebriated period turns creative writing itself into a crucible where notions of the cognitive and the expressive are renegotiated. To see this point quickly, consider the novel *Shame*, where Rushdie—or, if you prefer, the novel's narrator—notes that the forms of fantasy and fabulation come naturally if you do not have the rooted, self-assured knowledge claims over the society you write about that the classical nations with continuous primordial identities used to regard as the natural stance to be taken by their novelists. In other words, Indian creative writing in English took off precisely when the climate of creative writing put a certain cognitive framing exercise in power, and the expressive needs of expatriate and other identity-insecure Indians met the newly available formal devices, which we may abbreviate under the rubric of metafiction.

These successes in metacreative writing by NRIs roughly synchronise with the high-profile NRI presence in Silicon Valley, in particular, and the emergence of the professional NRI profile in the West in general—an emergence whose domestic incidence in India, in the educational sector as brain drain and in the home lives of affluent families as the partial export of their work force, correspondingly transformed the Indian social scene around the same time, in ways that are only beginning to be taken seriously. It seems fair to say that the literary centre of gravity of the high writing in English by Indians lies today in the NRI base of the Indian anglophone community. What if this community is best viewed as being on its way to building a self-definition, an identity if you wish, from the industrial base it already has rather than the popular-cultural base which its India-resident fraction lacks? What if the project of such an identity building can complete itself, becoming reflexive and self-reproducing, without incorporating the rural base of an Indian nation along the lines of the nations imagined earlier? What would such a development, so read, do to our understanding of what is happening, and what sorts of outcome are possible?

We bear such questions in mind as we visualise ways in which the project of anglophone Indian identity construction can move towards completion.

Scenarios of bounded completion

Our first exercise is to note ways in which such completion can occur that involve forming a strong boundary between the haves in India, who speak English fluently and marketably (differentiated into various markets, including some with a non-market self-image, in the literary sector), and the have-nots. We shall visualise scenarios, then, of a bounded completion of the task of anglophone identity construction.

One such scenario proposes a frank sellout to an exogenous master elite or to several such elites calling the shots. There are variants, depending on the master elite's being white or of Indian origin, on different geopolitical fractions of such a master elite being successfully played off against each other by an agile India-based comprador elite or receiving uniform servility, and other obvious considerations.

The other scenarios are couched in the nationalist rhetoric. I would argue that they all involve hypothecating this nation to a master narrative, and that they differ only on their choice of narrative. This of course is an empirical thesis and deserves criticism and testing. With some misgivings, we may appropriate the mainstream terms 'right' and 'left', speaking of the left narrative scenario, which conducts its serious discourse in English alone (and, rather strikingly, never did learn enough German and Russian for that to make a difference), as distinct from the right narrative scenario, whose serious discourse, though conducted in English, allocates specific roles to a Sanskrit sublexicon (even in its English) and to the Hindi language as an arena of narrative anchorage. On our analysis, the national political parties on the right and on the left are equally committed to the articulation in English alone of the knowledge base of India—and, we argue, to the emergence of an English-focused core elite—with respect to a particular master narrative driving the key discourses. The parties differ only in that they choose different master narratives.

The frank sellout scenario and the two nationalist scenarios (the left narrative and the right narrative) all count as visualisations of bounded completion for the project of constructing an identity for the anglophone Indian elite. They all involve fortifying the walls separating this elite from the Indian public as a whole. They all reject India's modern languages as sites for the redefinition of modernity through public conversations relative to specific regions, for they assume tacitly that modernity is a given, flowing from either a master elite in some West or a master narrative in some epistemological heaven.

Concrete implementations of such programmes will of course play ball with India's regional languages and the political forces representing them. It is a matter of containing them as special interest groups, a problem that such a programme will also need to address in the case of categories like dalits or adivasis or women. The idea will be to hand out various types of populist sops and to appear to give these local specifications a place of honour in the grand scheme that the master narrative weaves. One would predict that, once such containment is successful, the relevant constituency's distinctive language, if any, will be re-sanskritised via English as the new Sanskrit, ever willing to purify local power into a representation of central power.

On any of the bounded completion scenarios, one must visualise not only the political actions and their dynamics but also the journalistic and academic commentary that stages and shapes them. Thus, one imagines a dispassionate, spectatorial mainstream social science community looking on, possibly pleading for some sort of modern or antirevivalist outcome when it takes sides at all, but underwriting a consensual view of the spectrum of choices available as ranging from sellout through right nationalism to left nationalism, period. Further, when we think about the possible sanskritisation of properly contained local satrapies, we cannot help also imagining a certain mainstream social science adding to the event itself the commentarial *masala* of an academically worded celebration of the victory of rational, communication-maximising, modern forces of civil sentiment over the primordial subject matter of a nineteenth century ethnology.

We turn now to another spectrum of possibilities.

Programmes of sustainable repletion

This section features another way to visualise the task of strengthening the Indian public's base of modern knowledge to the point at which one feels that this public is as much of a learner as any other community of learners—what one might consider a completion or a phase transition. On the conception considered here, one would speak, however, not of completion, but of a certain type of repletion. The idea is that the community reaches a point in its management of the relevant resource (here, knowledge as a resource) where its members know how to replenish whatever items get exhausted. If these members are confident about reproducing and upgrading such know-how through further phase transitions, it is possible to speak specifically of sustainable repletion. The main point is to consider scenarios that ask what things look like if India counts as a knowledge-producing site rather than a site merely of distribution and consumption.

We consider here agendas that ask how this goal can be attained with the whole Indian public as the relevant domain rather than just some elite defined in terms of differential possession of some scarce resource such as fluent knowledge of English. Of course, such agendas allow that the public goal of repletion with respect to knowledge resources may involve certain private subgoals. Thus, it is not surprising if a subcommunity that speaks only or mainly English, in the course of pursuing its own subgoals of reproduction and expansion, turns out to be serving the public interest as far as knowledge resources are concerned, for example, by becoming model textbook writers or schoolteachers. But things change for such a subcommunity, say the anglophone Indians, if its articulate members view these private subgoals in the matrix of the public goal of replenishing knowledge resources and manage to work in terms of such a view as well as to communicate it—not necessarily in these conceptual terms, but possibly by revisiting familiar Gandhian notions of trusteeship—to their constituencies. We consider here the possibility of certain articulators of the anglophone Indian community's interests moving into a visualisation of this type.

The conceptual content of such a transition is perhaps most usefully summarised as a shift from the model of a 'master narrative qua foundation' to the countermodel of a 'host narrative qua arena'. The strategic issue for such a transition may be phrased roughly as follows: will India's English writers be able to write up the hybrid non-site of open negotiation as an achievement screenplay? For only if the appearance of workaholic frenzy is reproduced, will the key actors in anglophone India's social field consent to participate in accomplishing such a transition. The problem is that a hybrid non-site where you relativise certain cultures to others does not immediately look like a scene of heroic action.

An affirmative response to this strategic question may be forthcoming from the normal visualisers of such scenarios. If the social scientific advisors to the new prince, while they quarrel over the doses of subversion *masala* to be added to their recipes, hit upon a way to package sustainable relativisation as a success story in the new genre of negotiation, then we are home.

The word 'home' is not an inadvertent choice, of course. It designates the problem of sustainable relativisation of culture to culture in terms of the task of mutual hospitality, the challenge of finding ways for each culture to play both guest and host to the other. This strategic problem is in dialogue with central theoretical issues in social science to the extent that a communication-symmetrising concept of learning can be reconstrued in a mutualising fashion, in terms of extending reciprocal, cognitive hospitality as a level where the cognitive economy of culture is defined by the actual cycle of re-cognised, re-written, re-cultured practices circulating in a pattern of generalised reciprocity. Such a level seeks a new political science that crucially relativises sociology's industriality to anthropology's sustainable notion of cognitive transmission and provides a model, in the theoretical negotiation- gesture itself, for the other relativisations.

My take on this matter is a lay take, as I am not a social scientist. I would wager, though, that the way out is to explicitly speak of fashioning communities of literacy, and to use the literacy and education systems, coupled with a realignment of the commercial media, in doing so. Suppose academic and sociopolitical planners join forces and agree to tell the public speaking each language, 'Dear speakers of X, you and we are working together to fashion a community of literacy that cultivates language X as a medium and a site of human construction. This normative location is going to be the result of certain adult negotiations. We will decide which texts shall count as canonical for the pedagogy. This negotiated result will vary over time and space. We recognise that the choice of canon and of pedagogy will shape our children in particular ways, and we shall monitor what is happening to these children so that we can vary our policies intelligently. While the media shall be free, we will from now on seek some accountable linkage between pedagogy and the media. Let us be careful about all this from now on, for the consequences of cultural pollution will affect our children.' Once we are able to make this move of ecological responsibility, we take the future of our cultures in our hands, and make it explicit to the public that, while the acquisition of spoken language is natural, the world of writing is constructed. When we tell each other that that too is natural, we end up handing it over to the non-management of the market under piecemeal trouble-shooting by the state, which is no substitute for a scenario of seriously self-governing literate communities.

This was about management within each speech community, which is the site of crucial and formative action. However, my main concern here is with the relations between such communities. I, therefore, return to the affirmative packaging that anglophone India's articulators, including its pedagogic articulators, can be expected to create. On my take, the point is to articulate the way this subcommunity faces the Indian (non-anglophone) public and the global (anglophone) public in terms of the twin challenges of learning how to play guest and host. As a point of departure for the job of redefining these issues, let us consider the following proposal. In mainstream articulations, India's anglophone elite views itself as playing host to the rest of India and guest to the North (or to the Metropolis, or to the first world, however you put it). The new articulations that can now be expected to emerge will persuade it to self-consciously also play guest to the rest of India and host to the first world. This proposal enables us to see how programmes of sustainable repletion fan out into concrete options. There are options that stress the idea of learning how to play host to the first world. This is an old idea at one level. But we are already finding out that it is a new idea. To play host to anglophone whites coming to India is also a matter of learning how to help them learn to behave like real guests; this turns out to be linked to our own global task in the third world. As we continue to grow with other third world countries into a politically articulate understanding of the role all of us have been playing in letting the first world take off into the consumerist stratosphere at our expense, it will become easier to spell out the variants of the programme that stress learning how to play host to the whites.

Other options emphasise the component of learning how to play guest, and not host, to the non-anglophone 'rest of India'. Institutionally, this means relativising the work done at the university departments of English to the study of the Indian habitat that has, in various non-English languages, received and recast the literature and culture of the industrial and managerial leviathan. I am happy to report that this relativisation is already happening, thanks to cultural studies, feminism and other radicalities, and that one can expect it, in a decade or two, to do its own self-conscious work in the Indian languages which will crucially reshape such agendas. Yet another set of options focuses on the industrial hijack of the cognitive and seeks to reverse it in practice while elaborating the terms of this reversal in the theoretical commentary accompanying this practice. This deeper relativisation of industry to non-industry, of English to non-English, asks directly the question of what form the industrial-English hijack has taken and what one is supposed to do about it in order to arrive at sustainable repletion levels for knowledge resources, given that such a hijack is not sustainable. In this variant, the programme must pursue the general negotiation of the formal sector of all economies, including the cognitive economy, with the informal sector that surrounds it and must underwrite it for its formalities to be sustainable. Here one looks forward to a more clearly articulated alliance of feminism, ecology, aboriginal rights and a geographically focused, possibly district-level regionalism that will reformulate the basic questions of who knows what, and who learns what from whom in the domain of resources and management. Such a recast localist struggle will lead to a redefinition of the idea of economics to which the social sciences have mortgaged human rationality.

All these variants of the programme depend on the powers and limits of narrative for the possibility of becoming properly tellable stories of anglophone India's search for a dignified identity without a particular piece of land. Current writing shows that narrative can celebrate unfinishable but sustainable negotiation as richly as it can the older goal of permanent-looking victories over various adversaries. Only in and after such new narratives can the English-focused expressive cluster of Indians in and outside India get their act together. It is then that all the scenarios and programmes considered in this argument are likely to get a hearing.

Concluding, unscientific postscript

This is a methodological remark about the human studies and the social sciences, and addresses the question of how the various modes of discourse in our interwoven disciplines can and cannot add up. I begin with the double articulation of modern society in what I might call the literature of narrative and the numerature of head counts and measurements of relative might, following the divide between literacy and numeracy in the qualitative and quantitative academic disciplines respectively. These two articulations meet at the point of discursive knowledge. The human studies look at the invitational core content of a narrative community, examining how this content—the community inviting the new and the other into its self—narrates and thus constitutes itself as a continuity. The social sciences consider how such content is consumed, distributed and limited, formulating their speculations in a form that takes off from a journalistic ground and flaps its numerate wings in a scientific sky. This genre feeds back into the journalistic and narrative enterprises, activating an endless cycle of hybridisation that neither the social studies nor the human sciences can ever hope to understand, but only to sustain, if we wish to continue to clothe our discursive knowledge in such shapes.

There are other choices to consider. The present paper has argued against the picture of a natural presence of English (as a code) in India (as a place). Those who wish to reiterate their arguments for the naturalness of primordial loyalties and the residues of history are of course welcome to the debate. As an opponent of the worship of products, I am doctrinally bound to welcome their process as yet another guest in Processland, even if their preference is to defend the reality of products instead, packaging them as pieces of nature herself. As a television commercial put it in the seventies, 'Milk is a natural, milk is a natural.' I will be happy to argue against that position if my colleagues want me to, with the necessary amusement, which I hope I will be forgiven for.

7

The Role of English and Language Teaching in Switzerland

Stefano Vassere

Introduction

This article aims to provide a primary analysis of information relevant to the English language and the way in which it increasingly occupies a problematic position in relation to a quadri-linguistic system that is regarded as a sociolinguistic model like that of Switzerland. The system guarantees noteworthy protection of local minority languages. For example, a relatively small community such as that of Italian-speaking Switzerland (3 million speakers in the traditional area of the language in a national reality of approximately 7 million inhabitants) can rely on a significant recognition of its language in terms of being able to conduct daily public activities exclusively in Italian; in being able to have access to electronic media in Italian through State concessions; and in being able to count on the validation of this language through the relationship that exists with the central administration of the confederation. In a system where school policies are locally designed by the various cantons, the promotion of the national languages that fall outside of their own territory appears most problematic, precisely where the need to learn English at least during the years of obligatory schooling is the most urgent and concrete. In these situations, cantonal schools are tempted to reform, if not otherwise to completely eliminate, the teaching of at least one national language (the third language), and in some cases even the second national language.

In an attempt to identify the principal tendencies of a phenomenon where the role of the English language has become decisive in the re-discussion of the power relationship which for much time was consolidated, the analysis in this article will be based on the consideration of the twenty different school curricula present in the three principal regions of the country.

Switzerland

Switzerland is a confederation of 26 states that consist of 20 cantons and 6 semi-cantons. Each state has its own legislative power this is administered through a one-chamber parliament called the Grand Council, and its own executive power, the State Council. The confederation itself has a two-chamber parliament (a 'popular' chamber, known as the National Council, and a chamber of cantons, called the Council of the States). Each state has, to a greater or lesser degree, freedom over a series of competencies, such as healthcare, public order on a cantonal level, culture and education. The defence force and administration of state companies, amongst others, are the responsibility of the confederation.

Switzerland has a population of approximately 7.3 million, of which 20.5% are foreigners. Within the foreign community, 24% are from the ex-Yugoslavian state, 22% from Italy, 9% from Portugal, 1.8% from Germany, 6% from Spain, 6% from Turkey, 4% from France, 9% from the rest of Europe and 12% from other continents. Four languages are constitutionally recognised: German (63.7% of the overall population), French (20.4%), Italian (6.5%) and Romansh (0.5%). The rights of the national minority languages are guaranteed by precise articles of the federal constitution[1], and the

[1] The current constitutional text on languages in Switzerland is divided into different articles. A1 'First Title: General Regulations', Article 4 'National Languages' states: 'German, French, Italian and Romansh are the national languages.' 'Second Title: Fundamental Rights, Civil Rights and Social Objectives', in 'Chapter 1: Fundamental Rights', Article 18 states that 'the freedom of language is guaranteed', while 'Chapter 2: Competencies', 'Section 3: Training, research and culture', Article 70, defines the Federal linguistic relationships in more detail. Article 70, 'Languages': (a) The official languages of the confederation are German, French and Italian. Romansh is the official language when dealing with people who speak Romansh. (b) Each canton chooses its official language. To maintain linguistic peace, each canton respects the traditional language composition of the region and respects indigenous minority languages. (c) The confederation and the cantons promote understanding and exchange between linguistic communities. (d) The confedera-

propagation of national languages is territorial in nature (there is a German Switzerland, French Switzerland, Italian Switzerland and, in part, a Romansh Switzerland).

National and non-national languages: the principal language

The degree to which foreigners are integrated into Swiss society is large, and can be measured by the percentage of foreigners who consider a national language as a principal language (62.3% in 2000).

In the year 2000, the percentage of people who considered a non-national language as a principal language was approximately 9%; at the time, Switzerland had a count of forty languages, each with over 1000 speakers. The more widely spoken of these languages were: Serbia-Croatian (1.4%), Albanian (1.3%), Portuguese (1.2%), Spanish (1.1%) and English (1%). English was considered a principal language by 0.4% of the Swiss. Within the group of non-national languages, English represented 9.9% of the sample. Of the people who considered English a principal language, 52.9% lived in German Switzerland, 44.5% in French Switzerland, 2.6% in Italian Switzerland and 0.1% in Romansh Switzerland. These people lived principally in the major Swiss-German cities (Zurich and Basel) and on the banks of the Leman Lake (in French Switzerland). As stated, the majority of the people who considered English a principal language were foreigners.

National and non-national languages: their use in the family, at work and in school in 1990

With regard to the data relevant to the effective use of the languages (in contrast to the considerations on principal language and mother tongue), the only data available at present is that taken from the 1990 census[2] and some relevant to the year 2000. Concentrating solely on the propagation of foreign languages, we will notice that 13% of the Swiss population indicate a non-national language as a language used at home.

---

tion supports multilingual cantons in the carrying out of their special tasks. (e) The confederation supports the provisions made by the Grigioni and Ticino cantons to preserve and promote the Romansh and Italian languages.

[2]See Lüdi and Werlen (1997), where the data is reported and analysed in detail.

The importance of English is noteworthy when one considers that it is a language used in the workplace. In 1990 the use of English in the workplace or at school was 17.4% in the German region of Switzerland[3], 13% in the French region[4], and 7.8% in the Italian region. It is important to note that in the French region the use of English (13%) in the workplace is more than the use of German (11.7%), which is a national language[5], while in the German region, French maintains a marginal lead (19.2% as opposed to 17.4%)[6]. The percentages relevant to the Italian region present themselves in the following order: German (17.5%), French (14.8%) and English (7%)[7]. Lüdi and Werlen (1997, 203–205) clarifies that the propagation of English is high in professional fields such as aviation, natural sciences, tourism, trust agencies, advertising and marketing—a situation that similarly extends itself to other regions of the country.

This data gives a clear idea of the propagation of English in Switzerland. Although the language is not represented strongly in the list of non-national languages regarded as mother tongue (where it only figures in the fifth place), it occupies an important place in the professional sector, where in all regions of the country it is represented as one of the three non-local languages used. In the two major regions, it is considered one of the two non-local languages, and in the French region, it is considered the first non-local language used in the professional sector[8].

With regard to the data relative to the federal census of 2000 (which does not present any data analysis but simply gives non-detailed statistics supplied by the Federal Statistics Office), one can deduce that the use of the different languages in the workplace and at school is configured in the following manner: in Switzerland, German is used by 75.8% of the active population, French by 36.5%, English by 19.2% and Italian by 12.3%. In German Switzerland, 98.2% use German, 21% English, 18.8% French and 10.2% Italian. In French Switzerland, 97.1% use French, 15.1% English,

[3]Lüdi and Werlen (1997, 152)
[4]Lüdi and Werlen (1997, 203)
[5]Lüdi and Werlen (1997, 203)
[6]Lüdi and Werlen (1997, 152)
[7]Bianconi (1995, 93)

13% German and 5.6% Italian. In Italian Switzerland, 97.8% use Italian, 18.4% German, 14.3% French and 9.2% use English.

Even in 2000, the data show a situation in which on the one hand in the whole of Switzerland and Italian Switzerland, English is always preceded by two national languages as used at the workplace and at school, and on the other hand, in German and French Switzerland, English is by now the second language after the language used in the region (German in German Switzerland and French in French Switzerland).

The teaching of language

It is clear that this situation would have implications to the teaching of national and non-national languages in canton schools which, as stated earlier, function according to local legislative systems. The need for the promotion of the teaching of English is not only strongly felt in the economic sector but by the students themselves and their families who increasingly request that English be taught with a purpose and at an early age. It thus becomes apparent that these tendencies begin to impose themselves on a linguistic education system that has until recently had to take into consideration a 'baggage' of national languages that is already extremely full. If one considers, for example, the case of Italian, the third language of the country, one will notice that between the necessity to teach the two major languages (notwithstanding that they are important international languages at least in Europe) on the one hand, and that of having to produce a curriculum that takes into consideration the consistent teaching of English on the other, the latter does nothing but markedly increase the burden to fulfil a study plan on students who will find themselves up against having to intensely learn three languages until fifteen years, without forgetting to study the Italian language in depth as it is their mother tongue. If one then takes into consideration the high percentage of foreigners entering the country, one begins to understand that for certain students Italian itself is a foreign language, and in their case, the number of foreign languages to study becomes four.

---

[8]For the German and Italian regions, see Lüdi – Werlen (1997, 391–400)

In the light of these problems, over the last few years, Switzerland has opened a noteworthy debate regarding the teaching of languages. If French Switzerland tends to be privy to a system of language teaching that presents the teaching of English and German contemporaneously, with German in a privileged position with respect to English, German Switzerland tends to privilege English over French. A further difficulty is the case apparent in Italian Switzerland where the community itself is Italian in terms of regional territoriality, and the language itself is spread over the entire national territory.

The interests echoed with reference to a general teaching of English in schools across the country are moreover those specific to industry, global economy and the requests of employers rather than those of the students and their parents. Furthermore, (although the idea until now seems only partially developed) there is a tendency to begin to think in terms of English as the lingua franca within the Swiss community itself[9]. There is, furthermore, a more general interest that takes into consideration the fact that in certain environments of the community the tendency is to believe that without a generalised introduction to English, Switzerland will remain isolated from the international community.

General tendencies

The present situation in relation to the teaching of English is one that is in continuous evolution. More than half of the Swiss school-going population learns English as a second or third foreign language. (From this point onwards the term foreign language will be used to indicate a learnt language that is not the language of the community. Thus, German, French and Italian, although national languages, are considered foreign languages from the point of view of the two linguistic communities that do not share the languages.) However, the requests that are prevalent regarding the teaching of English tend towards the temporal prioritising of its teaching

[9]If one takes this point of view, it is evident that the option of introducing English as a national language of communication would also have to take into consideration the development of new structural and grammatical rules in terms of this language, including terminology that is exclusively Swiss to describe and name objects, concepts and institutions that are Swiss by nature. It is at this point that the issue of a

in schools before the teaching of the other languages. In certain cantonal projects, there is a tendency to introduce the teaching of English at the primary school level. Two fundamental points on which the present debate is based are (a) at what stage in the process of compulsory schooling should English be introduced, and (b) should English replace French as a first foreign language in German Switzerland (notwithstanding that, for the moment, in French Switzerland, the decision has been taken to teach German first)[10].

The present general tendencies, as stated before, are evolving with a certain amount of speed. Until three years ago, the teaching of English was of interest only at the eighth and ninth year of school, in exceptional cases at the seventh year. Since 2002, almost all the cantons (for approximately four-fifth of the total number of students) decided to systematically advance the obligatory teaching of English to the seventh year. Furthermore, recent indications that emerged from the Swiss conference of Cantonal Directors of Public Education (CDEP) are suggestive of an invitation to the various cantons to provide for the teaching of English in primary schools, from the first five or six years of obligatory schooling.

Brief analysis of the factors raised

The factors raised by the scientific debate on the teaching of the English language (factors that are worth returning to) are in fact arguments of a linguistic, economic and pedagogic nature and centre around linguistic politics[11]. Arguments that are of a linguistic nature very often cross paths with those that are exclusively of a pedagogic nature and refer to the preferences of students in terms of language learning. These preferences were measured through opinion surveys. Thus, according to one recent survey, English is

---

linguistic norm comes to the fore, as in certain circles the idea of 'pan Swiss English' is already prevalent (Watts and Murray 2001, 3).

[10]In truth, the situation is far more complex, in as much as one should take into account, for example, the number of hours and the financial resources that a canton invests in the teaching of a single language (in merit one refers back to Grin 2000). One must also add that still in 1990, 70% of the cantons declared themselves in favour of a national language to be taught as a first foreign language in schools.

[11]Stauffer (1999, 62–65).

regarded as the ideal language to be taught as a first foreign language, while another survey shows that French is regarded as the ideal language to be taught as a first foreign language. Other means of measurement are related to the ability to auto-validate linguistic competency.

Economic factors are often raised by those who wish to promote the obligatory teaching of English. These factors can be noticed in companies and their attitudes towards employees. Recent studies (Grin and Vaillancourt 2000, Grin 2001) demonstrate that the degree of English competence in the workplace of German Switzerland (the majority region in Switzerland) is directly proportional to the salary earned. This does not seem to be the case in the other regions, namely the French and Italian ones. In these regions, the value of the national languages is equivalent, if not superior, to that of English.

The argument raised in terms of language politics centres round the promotion of a discourse that tends to safeguard the relationship and accord between the different linguistic communities in the country. To give up the 'priority' teaching of one or two of the national languages could, according to some, diminish the degree of linguistic, cultural, social and political exchange between the different regions of Switzerland. It is precisely on this point that those who advocate the option of English as the inter-language of communication in Switzerland strengthen their argument—an argument that up until now has not received any concrete proof or scientific valuation and does not seem to be practised in a systematic manner, not even in limited sectors of public life.

Central recommendations

The present situation is as delineated by the CDEP in a document of March 2004[12]. In this instance, the inter-cantonal body sets priorities with regard to the teaching of languages. The various cantons are then invited to adhere to these priorities. Besides focusing on the teaching of the language of the community (German in the case of German Switzerland, French in French Switzerland, etc.), a great deal of attention is also given to the teaching of foreign lan-

[12]EDK(2004)

guages. Here one begins to note the dispositions of the European Union regarding the teaching of two foreign languages and the willingness of Switzerland to adhere to this argument with an ear to the ground in the context of its federal structure and multilingual confederation. Particular attention is given to the 'potential of early language learning'. It is for this reason that the recommendations tend towards three principal priorities: the decisive promotion of the first language (mother tongue)[13]; the teaching of a second national language at the primary school level; and the teaching of another language (by rule English) in primary schools[14].

The time to put these changes into practice is fast approaching. Within two years, students will have to learn a second national language from the fifth year of school and English from the seventh. In the long term (by 2010 or 2012), provision will have to be made to teach two foreign languages, the first from the third year of school and the second from the fifth, and of these languages, one must be a national language.

This significant shift in the teaching of languages in schools cannot ignore the necessity to redefine the structures and didactic means at one's disposal. In the light of the latter, the CDEP is taking upon itself the responsibility of recommending the development of training courses for teachers and the reformulation of didactic and scientific research methods relevant to the training. Through this plan of action, it hopes to focus attention on the individuation of learning standards. The 'harmonisation' of the three cantons is envisaged in three periods: the beginning, the middle and the end of the period of learning. In addition to this, careful attention will be given to the formation and periodic evaluation of teachers and their abilities, the portfolio of individual linguistic competencies based

[13]We will indirectly allude to the problems surrounding the noteworthy number of dialects present in German Switzerland, which are frequently used in the greater part of public life (even if they are not yet indicated in formal register and writing). We will also note that developmental methods and modes of teaching that are based on *standard* language are more relevant to German Switzerland than other parts of the community.

[14]A certain amount of attention must also be given with regard to the languages of immigration which, as has been mentioned, represent a reality of Swiss multilinguism that cannot be undervalued. The CDEP has also made recommendations for the safeguarding of these languages.

on European standards, the introduction of management bodies regulating linguistic exchange, and the establishment of a centre of national linguistic competence.

The situation in the various linguistic regions

With regard to what has been briefly illustrated above, the CDEP and the different cantons have decided to subdivide the national reality into four homogenous compartments, making it the responsibility of one of these subdivisions to respond to the needs of the different linguistic curricula of each individual region. A great number of regional groups have signed agreements and formal declarations in this regard.

In the French and Italian regions of Switzerland ('Conférence intercantonale de l'instruction publique de la Suisse romande e du Tessin', Cantons Bern, Fribourg, Geneva, Jura, Neuchâtel, Vaud, Valais, Ticino), by formal declaration on 30 January 2003, German is to be the first language, learnt from the third year of school. The teaching of English is envisaged for the fifth year. In the canton of Ticino (Italian Switzerland), the teaching of French is envisaged from the third to the seventh year of school, German from the seventh to the ninth, and English from the eighth to the ninth year.

In the north-western German region of Switzerland ('Nordwestschweizerische Erziehungsdirektorenkonferenz', Cantons, Aargau, Bern, Basel Land, Basel Stadt, Fribourg, Luzern, Solothurn, Zurich), in the absence of a formal declaration, the tendency is towards the maintenance of French as the first foreign language.

In the central German region of Switzerland ('Bildungsdirektoren-Konferenz Zentralschweiz', Cantons Luzern, Nidwalden, Obwalden, Schwyz, Uri, Zug, Valais), on 20 June 2001, a decision was taken to introduce English from the third year of school, and French from the fifth.

In the German region of Switzerland and the principality of Liechtenstein ('Erziehungsdirektoren-Konferenz der Ostschweizer Kantone und des Fürstentums Liechtenstein', Cantons Appenzell Innerrhoden, Appennzell Ausserrhoden, Glarus, Grigioni, St Gallen, Schaffhausen, Thurgau, Zurich, and the principality of Liechtenstein), as per formal declaration of 29 October 2002, English is introduced from the third year of school, and French from the fifth.

Conclusion

The role of the English language within the sociolinguistic system of Switzerland is of primary importance, not so much in terms of a principal language, but rather with regard to its value at the workplace and as a language learnt at school. The data available in relation to 'mother tongue' shows that the majority of English speakers live in the German and French regions of Switzerland—the two principal regions of the country; less than 3% live in the Italian region. These represent less than a tenth of the people who declare a non-national language a principal language. In the major regions of the country, English is already considered a first language at the workplace, after the language of the region.

This situation has evident repercussions on the system of language teaching that is conducted on a regional basis. In this regard, one needs to state that the different Swiss regions are characterised by different attitudes towards the teaching of languages: in French and Italian Switzerland, the tendency is to favour and give preference to at least one of the national languages; this tendency is not shared by German Switzerland. All regions are, however, characterised by a rapid evolution in terms of the system of language teaching, and this is one of the reasons why the present situation does not appear to be very stable.

Evidently, the diffirences in the attitudes to and the teaching of languages do pose a problem in terms of cohesion and 'linguistic peace' within the country. There are potential problems of mobility, as for instance, the moving from one canton to another by a family with school-going children could entail a change in linguistic curriculum. In many cases, in fact, it is quite a substantial change. Given the situation, the region that is most penalised is the Italian region that has taken upon itself to teach English together with two major national languages.

References

Bianconi S. a cura di. 1995. *L'italiano in Svizzera. Secondo i risultati del Censimento federale della popolazione 1990*. Bellinzona: Osservatorio linguistico della Svizzera italiana.

Bianconi S. – Borioli M. a cura di. 2004. *Statistica e lingue. Un'analisi dei dati del Censimento federale della popolazione 2000*. Bellinzona: Ufficio di statistica.

EDK 2004. *Weiterentwicklung des Sprachenunterrichts: Gesamtschweizerischer Fahrplan festgelegt.* Bern: Schweizerische Konferenz der kantonalen Erziehungsdirektoren.

Grin F. and F. Vaillancourt 2000. On the Financing of Language Policies and Distributive Justice. In Phillipson R. ed. *Rights on Language: Equity, Power and Education.* New York: Lawrence Erlbaum Associates.

Grin F. 2001. *Der ökonomische Wert der englischen Sprache.* In R.J. Watts and H. Murray. 2001. 105–120.

Lüdi G. and I. Werlen. 1997. *Le paysage linguistique de la Suisse.* Bern: Office fédéral de la statistique.

Stauffer M. 1999. *Aspects du Concept général pour l'einseignement des langues. Résultats d'une enquête IDES en Suisse et dans la principauté du Liechtenstein.* Bern: Conférence suisse des directeurs cantonaux de l'instruction publique.

Watts R. J. and H. Murray. 2001. Die fünfte Landessprache? Englisch in der Schweiz, Zürich: vdf Hochschulverlag AG in der ETH.

8

A Second Look at English as a Window on the World That Has Changed

Jacob Tharu

The very fact of an international seminar on the theme of collaboration in teaching English is an indication of the importance of English as a world language today. I would draw into the emblematic value of this conclave the energy, enthusiasm and optimism we share in addressing issues (prospects rather than problems) in a pragmatic 'action' space. This mood reflects a growing sense that English is a material resource that can be harnessed and deployed for a range of purposes, especially for the expanding transactions riding on modern communication technology that mark our comfortable transition into the information age. My observations in this paper stem from a concern about the danger of being so mesmerised by the more visible and certainly appealing aspects of the usefulness, efficiency and profitability of communication through English that much of its true richness as a language of the wider world moves out of focus and so is not appreciated and engaged with. I do not suggest that English as a language per se is in any way superior to the many languages of our region. The focus here is on the varied advantages that having English available as an *additional* language carries for countries/societies of the outer circle (Kachru 1986).

English and ELT in the first half century after Independence

The major consideration in preserving a role for English in secondary and post-secondary education, including—significantly—the expanding public education sector, in newly independent India was its utility as a means of access to 'knowledge', especially of recent and ongoing developments in various disciplinary areas related to the modernisation project. I note in passing that the status of English as an official language for national level administration and inter-state communication was intended in the constitution to be a temporary arrangement. I take it that this 'window on the world' metaphor, representing the value of English, influenced policy relating to education in many other countries of the emerging third world of the fifties and sixties. In India, the notion of English as a library language had a determining influence on the formulation of goals and methodology for 'general English'. Curriculum development and teacher training for a reformulated general English (GE) at the high school, intermediate and first-degree levels constituted the mandate and indeed created the identity of the ELT profession in the first three decades or so after 1947.

The ideas I wish to share relate to English and perspectives on teaching English in the present age. Before that, I need to highlight a few points about ELT activity in the later part of the last century relating them to the status (used in a general sense here) of English. This section does not attempt a systematic history of ELT. The focus is more on the goals that guided English teaching, and not on the conceptual foundations of the curriculum and methodology. I take the central mandate of the ELT profession (which developed as a result of the training initiatives of the government through various agencies) to lie essentially in the sector of public education. I suggest that by the late 1960s this new field had been quite well established. These remarks relate to the constituency of public education, rather than to the segment of society that patronises and thrives on the private English-medium school. There is a top layer of English-using 'professionals' who are marked by an urban, middle-class social background and a personal history of education in a well-established private English-medium school, a premier college or an IIT, and probably a prestigious postgraduate degree in management. While these persons as students have probably benefited from modern ideas relating to developing communication skills, there is very little that teachers and syllabus makers specially trained in ELT have given them directly through courses in English.

English, then, for the vast majority of students was almost entirely a classroom related phenomenon—bounded by lessons, syllabus and examinations. English newspapers, movies, signboards, labels on consumer goods, and the like, might have created a haze in medium and small towns, but certainly nothing like an atmosphere marked by the language. The white-collar jobs available (potentially at least) were mainly in the clerical cadre. Students getting training in typing and shorthand while studying at the high school and intermediate levels was fairly common. For those proceeding to higher education, the push towards widening the use of regional languages as the medium of instruction during those decades meant that GE had no real academic relevance in the heavily populated arts faculties of state universities. Study skills did make a useful appearance occasionally in the English syllabus for science and technology students. It is a curious fact that English never featured in medical education—neither GE nor ESP. The gateway to salaried and stable jobs was the series of competitive examinations conducted by the Staff Selection Commission, Banking Service Recruitment Boards, LIC, Railway Service Commissions, etc. (The Pradesh Service Commission examinations did not have an English paper.) The English component of these national-level examinations supported a huge coaching industry, for which grammar exercises and guess questions (with model answers, of course) for writing tasks formed the staple. Qualifying at these examinations was the big concern relating to English, not the acquisition of skills to any worthwhile degree. It is worth noting here that after objective type tests became a norm, following the lead of the UPSC's civil services prelims, reading skills did get a boost. The passages for comprehension and for the cloze sub-test were all 'unseen', and they did demand more comprehension than the old precis passage. Coaching classes had to provide more reading practice, as memorising answers to expected questions became irrelevant. (The regular teaching of GE in schools and colleges, of course, continued unshaken.)

This modest emphasis on reading ability apart, there was no pressure to develop communication skills: neither from the examination schemes nor from the world beyond the examinations. Jobs where English skills apparently mattered were mainly in the private sector, with less open selection procedures, and for which anyway the pool of candidates from English medium schools alone was already too large. Boys and girls from government schools were nowhere in the running.

This is not in any sense a complete picture. The note of gloom, if apparent, is altogether unintended. The attempt here is to capture the elements in this wider setting that had an impact on the teacher of GE. I am focusing specifically on teachers at the secondary and post-secondary levels: typically, persons oriented through ELT programmes at the CIEFL and elsewhere. They were equipped with ideas and techniques to develop functional language skills (as against passing on information) and fulfil the mission of ELT. The pioneers (especially at the college level) faced two huge impediments. One was the syllabus which, suffused with the wisdom of the worthies who formed boards of studies, privileged the supposedly ennobling content of the prose and poetry selections embalmed in the prescribed readers—thus virtually ensuring that the examination remained the regurgitation-from-memory farce. The second was the blank wall of apathy, even resistance, from students. Most of them quite understandably saw no reason why, when guides for the examination were available in abundance, they should bestir themselves to work their way through several language exercises rather than sit back and enjoy the performance of the teacher. These virtuoso performances—elucidating the text with considerable erudition or describing the intricacies of the grammar and phonology of English—could be a lot of fun for the audience in the galleries. There was a third problem, a burden that the more enthusiastic teachers (those who had been 'converted' to language as it were) had to carry. This was a family affair. There were always colleagues who stayed faithfully with English main (literature), and who had for their poor language-teaching cousins, at best, pity for having to do such low grade work, and at worst, hostility for letting the side down. Life was tough at the front line of GE in the arts faculty. (And those noble foot soldiers formed my constituency for about three decades. They inspire this story.)

English in the new millenium

Fast forward to 2001 and the globalised today we now celebrate. I am sure there are others who have shown how the presence and value of English in our lives has expanded. I will only say cheekily here that though the medical transcription boom is over, many other good things are coming in its place. So there is no cause to worry. The significant features of the new situation for my broad argument are just two. One is the fact that English today means, for a significant proportion of people, *speaking* English with some attested effectiveness in the real world rather than passing a traditional, annual written examination. Satellite TV has no doubt been a major influence. Equally important, I submit, is the whole range of new types of jobs that came with liberalisation, globalisation and the rapid growth of the domestic IT-based sector. The critical element here is that a usable level of skill in using English is required. The large expansion in skilled and thus paying jobs has come in, what I term, the polytechnic-training-based jobs, rather than in the more exclusive university-degree-based fields of engineering and medicine. The NIIT and APTEC computer academies and the numerous hotel management training institutes are familiar examples. Business studies is now available in scores of B-schools, not in just a few IIMs. It is pertinent to recall here that the UGC had made a far-sighted move in this general direction as early as 1995. As part of the scheme for the vocationalisation of degree-level education, thirty-five subjects were identified for special curriculum development. English was one of them. This amounted to recognising that English skills had a productive value in themselves, which is quite different from treating it as the medium for work in other areas—the ESP model. Also, importantly, this teaching of 'vocational English' was to take place in the 'ordinary' arts college, not in special institutes.

There is a process of democratisation in progress here; and this is the second significant feature of the presence of English today. A job market and work force with a broad social base together with the prominence of spoken English skills at work has made the relevance of the language highly visible to large segments of the population. Hence the clamour for more English from ordinary people. The slogan *angrezi hatao* has been well and truly forgotten. In its place has come the policy of introducing English as a subject from class 1. Some observers dismiss this as a populist move and question its educational wisdom. But rather than hide behind the pedantry of 'wisdom', I think what we should do is examine the immediate feasibility of primary-level English in relation to the current desultory level of resource allocation for primary education—without simply accepting the latter as an unchanging given. An honest pedagogy can be worked out and put in place. To return to the main point, it is that this widespread and fairly direct contact with English in use is something new. English is no longer some remote but powerful mystery, lying hidden in the world of textbooks and examinations. It is an English that lives in sizeable tracts of urban India.

New possibilities for thinking about goals for teaching English

All that has been said so far has only been a rather long introduction. The simple and fairly obvious assertion to be made is that happy days are here for ELT. I now turn to my main argument, which stems, as mentioned earlier, from a concern that we might lose sight of the many and varied possibilities that English now holds. The notion of the 'window on the world' is re-invoked here, but it has to be updated. With English riding high on advertising-promoting consumerism, the old meaning of 'window' is perhaps no longer helpful. We are constantly besieged by pop-up windows on the computer monitor. The print holdings in university libraries no longer dominantly represent recent and fast-developing knowledge (or at least information potentially of use); it is the Internet we access. The post-secondary level or college-going student cast in the role of an information receiver (with a set syllabus as the boundary) is no longer the idealised learner/user around whose needs the post-secondary English syllabus is to be framed.

We are committed to the universalisation of elementary education. Whatever the limitations of the high-profile DPEP exercises during the 1990s, the notion of quality in public education is catching on; and it is being demanded by those for whom it matters. Resources are improving, though only very slowly. Teaching aids are no longer only a fleeting token gesture appearing in the BEd practical examination. The range available and accessible is substantial. Educational Satellite (EDUSAT) has just been launched. TV lessons and material on CDs can reach large numbers of rural schools, power outages notwithstanding. NGO involvement in education now often includes comprehensive programmes targeting schools in scores (even hundreds), not just small and isolated islands of innovation.

The provision now is for about ten years of English at school. Post-secondary GE can build on this base. The motivation to learn English is strong, fueled in large measure by a sense of rights grounded in democratic aspirations. The poor are not only dancing to the tune of demagogic politicians. Many of the features that made 'teaching English in difficult circumstances' (TEIDC) a productive theme of professional discourse in international ELT are not so pressingly near in India. I also note, again cheekily in passing, that summer courses to train us to cope better with TEIDC are not as readily available in the northern hemisphere as they once were. There is much that we can do with English, especially at the secondary and higher levels of education. Much more than we, as a profession, could dream was possible just two decades ago.

I am not about to unveil some grand futuristic vision. Indeed my position might appear retrograde. The essential idea is that serious attention to the development of the receptive skills in English can yield far-reaching individual and social benefits. Two claims are involved. One is that an emphasis on reading and listening is something new. The counter claim is obvious. Have we not been stuck with the library slogan for decades now? This is the point: it only remained a slogan. Any honest assessment of actual achievement of reading skills in English at the college entry level will show how abysmally poor the record is. It is true that our examination system has been an impediment. But that is not all. Our orientation to ability/skill in relation to English—what matters most—has also been a factor. Our hallowed tradition has as one main tenet the distinction between seen and unseen comprehension, which guarantees that reading skills attained after eight or more years of instruction will match that of neo-literates. Listening is of course always there as the necessary absorbent of incessant teacher talk; but it could be said that only the few who got as far as taking the TOEFL ever realised that listening is a skill.

Privileging the receptive skills goes against a deeply ingrained tradition in English teaching in India, and possibly in most of the

Commonwealth too. There has been a massive neglect of this whole area at the level of curriculum transaction. Exercises and drills dealing with grammar and pronunciation take up a huge proportion of class time. These activities demanding production/performance were seen (not without some logic, but naïvely all the same) as the sure foundation for the productive skills of speaking and writing. Production-oriented tasks yield concrete and visible products that are more satisfying evidence to learners of gaining knowledge—of learning and progress—than what comes from progress in learning how to read. For the teaching establishment, production meant an abundance of riches by way of errors to be classified and corrected—again an easy and enormously satisfying source of evidence that teaching is occurring. (The reference here is to the teacher's own sense of usefulness and productivity, not to accountability demands from without.) All told, this focus on manageable little bits of the target language provided reassurance that we are getting closer to correct English, to good English, to the performance of the still-revered Englishman (neutralised as native speaker in the jargon of applied linguistics). The persistent neglect of the receptive skills, I suggest, did not just happen. Other priorities were inordinately high.

Emphasising receptive skills will thus not be an easily realised change in the way general English (for the masses) is handled. Perhaps clarifying that listening and reading require an active mind (despite silence and stillness) might help. In these days of learner-centred activity orchestrated by the teacher-facilitator, receptive processing is easily confused with passivity. Even where there is a commitment to communication skills, there is a tendency to assume that listening and reading will automatically be taken care of.

I take the strong position that a definite and fully committed focus on the development of the receptive skills of school-age learners of English can do more to help them consolidate and expand their language capabilities than the current priority given to production does. It is true that speaking ability has a high market value. I am not sure that what such focused training yields in the short term rests on a sound base of overall proficiency in the language. There is a lot of hype about presentation skills. The high profile and high paid among those with good speaking skills are for the most part producing seductive but inane and repetitive sales talk or performing as ventriloquists at call centres. The most important writing production the dynamic job hopper has to do is probably the confessional called the CV, for which the choice of downloadable templates which is bewildering. Where is communicative writing being practised? I am not suggesting that the productive skills are without any value and need not be developed. The heavy emphasis on them (experienced as burdensome and repetitive production tasks by the ordinary student in secondary school) can be relaxed without any lowering of eventual capability. (If nothing else, something should be kept in reserve so that English teachers at higher levels have work to do, errors to correct.)

The commitment to develop receptive skills called for here is ambitious; perhaps audacious. It means trying to teach reading and listening in a manner that would make learners interested in what they are exposed to, curious about learning more in an increasingly independent manner, and able to be critical. I do not believe any new methodology is needed. My 'complaint' relates essentially to errors of omission, not to inherent flaws in syllabus design and in teaching procedures. It also means, importantly, learners in their millions and not just the thousands from more privileged circumstances. An appreciation of the world now accessible easily (not exclusively) through English can help us gain the changed orientation being advocated here. It does not now represent only a supposedly superior civilisation (extolled in Macaulay's Minute), whose offerings/impositions we were prone to accept, given the asymmetric power relations that lasted for a century and a half after 'English education' came to us. It includes, importantly, our neighbours/friends in the countries of the South and East and those of the North that did not have a colonial presence in the third world. Neither the culture accessed through English, nor the language itself needs to be treated with awe. The latter shift in perspective makes for a tremendous liberation from the tongue-tying and pen-hand-cramping fixation on producing only correct forms from the word go. Teachers and learners can (a hope, not an injunction) now deal with English the way modern elementary school mathematics and science is approached.

To return to the newer world, the cultures (taken very broadly here) of our neighbours in the region are not easily available to us in our own languages. Learning more about and understanding them better (most conveniently through English) will become a concern as our economic and cultural ties get strengthened. This points to a wide range of 'content' that English readers and supplementary materials can easily hold. Handling such imaginatively can contribute to a more wholesome education, which in turn can help us grow out of our parochialism. I firmly reject the argument that the English curriculum (especially for the disadvantaged 'them') should be restricted to the familiar and the simple to avoid alienation. It is boredom that alienates, not stimulation and challenge.

Teaching reading well implies getting to the level of critical reading. Helping youngsters gain resources and confidence to adopt a critical stance is important. This will require effort and imagination on the part of teachers, and as a profession we need to foster a supportive climate. The capacity to be critical is important because the immediate world in English now is encountered primarily in an intrusive (pop-up) mode. Hence the need to develop the ability to resist gentle brainwashing into a complacent consumerism. We need to look through or beyond the front layer and see the richer world that exists and be proactive in engaging with it.

English will be a channel for promoting consumerism; increased productivity and profits will also be associated with acquiring English skills in a somewhat narrow technical manner. Together with this, English can contribute to the preparation of a better informed and more alert citizenry. As I have argued, the burden of being correct does not have to remain the first and insurmountable barrier to making the resource represented by English more democratically available.

A closing prayer

The ELT profession has an opportunity here to re-imagine its role and find meaning in contributing to a wholesome education for the many towards an empowered citizenship (besides aiding those who want to escape via the TOEFL and the IELTS). The ideal of more worthwhile education, with English as one important plank, is one that I am sure we share across national boundaries. This can be one starting point for exploring possibilities for collaboration.

References

Kachru, B. 1986. *The Alchemy of English. The Spread, Functions and Models of Non-native Englishes*. Oxford: Pergamon Press Ltd.

9

Equalising Access to English in Education and Balancing Multilingualism in India

E. Annamalai

Ubiquitous demand

The question whether English must find a place in school education in India has been answered positively by the various education commissions set up in India before and after Independence and in the educational policy formulated at various times by governments headed by political parties with different ideologies. English is the only constant in the nationwide implementation of the three language formula recommended by the national educational policy. Learning English by the general population through schools is one of the highly desired components of school education at the levels of the Union and the states. The unassailable position of English in schools in India is reflected in the fact that it is the only language taught throughout the country in almost all schools beyond the primary and to almost the entire population of students. English is learnt by students in 30.40 % of the primary schools in the country, 97.32% of the middle schools and 96.48% of secondary schools (NCERT 1999). Some of the Hindi states, which had dropped English from the school curriculum quickly restored it. The omnipresence of English in school education is unmatched by any Indian language; no Indian language (Hindi is a distant second) comes even near English in the number of learners of a second language. In recent years, English is taught outside the school system by more number of commercial and voluntary enterprises than any other Indian language, including Hindi. The consensus of ensuring a place for English in the school curriculum is derived from its elitist place in Indian multilingualism. It has special social and economic value in multilingualism because of its being the key to upward mobility in these domains. Its superior position in Indian multilingualism is reinforced by the growing global dominance of English in technology and business.

Divergent goals and methods

The question answered in different voices, however, is the *what* and *how* of teaching English. The *what* question divides into questions of content and objective. There are yet issues not reconciled in English education policy with regard to these questions. There is pedagogical agreement that the content of school English will be Indian, which, however, is yet to go beyond using the texts of Indian authors and having Indian names, festivals, events, myths and tales in the textbooks. At the same time, the policy equally emphasises the international importance and relevance of learning English, which implicitly recommends the English of the powerful English speaking country, which is the USA or the UK. This preference has increased recently when India has become dominant in providing IT driven services to the companies of these countries. This is more telling in call-service centres peopled by Indian graduates.

The problems of teaching English as a means of both intra-national communication and international communication are not yet adequately addressed. The policy prescription of teaching English as a library language, which involves imparting passive competence to support, supplement and enhance the knowledge acquired through an Indian language as recommended by the Indian Education Commission chaired by Kothari in 1968, further intensifies the problems. This policy, to begin with, does not sit well with the goal of imparting the active competence in English that is needed to use it as the language of spoken and written communication within and outside the country. These conflicting goals stem from differing individual goals of learners, partly shaped by their socioeconomic backgrounds. Not every learner of English, for example, aspires to be a scientist or to pursue higher education abroad. One way to reconcile the conflicting goals is to build in flexibility and diversification in the curriculum and the teaching methods of English in the country. Though such policy issues have great bearing on the 'how' question, they are not the focus of this paper.

With regard to the 'how' question, narrowed down to the method, the popular answer of having total immersion, or using English as the medium of instruction for all subjects in the curriculum except the mother tongue of the students, is unworkable and is unsupported by educational research (Crawford 1995, Cummins 1998)—in spite of the acclaimed success of the St Lambert experiment in Montreal (Lambert and Tucker 1972) and Prabhu's Bangalore–Madras Communicational Teaching Project[1] (Prabhu 1987) done under socioeconomic and sociolinguistic conditions, which are different from the conditions the large majority of students in India come from. This way of teaching the English language through its use as the medium of instruction, which is misperceived to be an effective method by the majority of parents, is not discussed further in this paper (see Annamalai 2004). The 'how' question discussed in this paper is with regard to teaching English as a language (that is, as a subject).

Early-start fallacy

This 'how' question divides into two parts, viz., when the teaching of English must start, and what the relationship of its teaching is with the mother tongue or the regional language taught in the school. With regard to when the teaching of English must end, the general agreement as reflected in educational policies is that it must continue to the end of schooling including higher secondary school or junior college. English is not taught for the whole duration of undergraduate education and professional education and is commonly reduced to one year. The focus in the teaching of English at the college level is literature in the name of students learning the aesthetic aspects of the language. Without a good foundation in the basic communicative skills in a language, the development of skills

[1]Prabhu's experiment is not an immersion programme in its technical sense, but is a method of teaching English through expressing meanings, which means learning any subject, or its meanings, by using English. When the range of meanings to express is to be broad, all subjects need to be mediated through English. This makes this programme closer to total or partial immersion.

for its aesthetic uses will be fruitless; at best, it could give passive skills to comprehend the aesthetic expressions of the language.

With regard to when the teaching of English must begin, the view that is gaining wider acceptance in government policy is that it must start as early as possible when schooling begins, which is increasingly class 1 (it begins commonly from pre-school only in private schools). Some parents take efforts to start English from home itself. The acceptance of the early start of English is shared by state governments irrespective of the political ideology of the party in power, whether it is Marxism (of the Communist Party in West Bengal), Free Market Socialism (of the Congress in Maharashtra, which is the latest state to join the rank from the academic year 2005–06) or cultural symbolism (of the Dravidian parties in Tamilnadu, which is moving in this direction). The view of early start is based on the assumption that longer exposure to a language gives better mastery of it. Though this assumption is valid in a general way as it is for any subject, it is contingent on other factors such as the quality of teaching, the qualification of teachers and the background of students. It may also affect learning other languages in terms of availability of curricular time. The latter cost is not about the issue of language load, or how many languages a child can learn simultaneously, which is empirically a misperception even in a formal instructional context (Srivastava et al. 1978). It is about pedagogical efficiency, which is taken up below.

Inadequate human resource

With regard to quality of teaching, the enormity of the number of teachers needed to teach English from class 1 is a challenge never to be met. There are 5,70,455 primary schools in India, of which 89% are in rural areas (NCERT 1999). The prescribed minimum qualification for the job of the primary school teacher is higher-secondary school, which does not give her sufficient proficiency in speaking or writing English and consequently in teaching it. The percentage of people with self-declared knowledge of English in the 1991 census is 11.15%—8% as a second language known after the mother tongue and 3.15% as a third language—Bhattacharya 2002). The percentage of students who complete school is 11% of the population of the country, and a little more than half of them,

6% of the population, go to college. (Probe Team 1999). The percentages of those who complete secondary school, and who declare that they have knowledge of English correspond. But these people cannot be considered to have adequate knowledge of English required to teach it. The percentage of students who successfully complete three years of college, which can be considered, at the risk of being liberal, to have a passable level of passive skills in English may constitute (by a conservative estimate of 10% of failures) about 5% of the population. If they are considered to have good enough skills in English to teach it, the percentage translates into 5,00,00,000 people (of a population close to 100,00,00,000 people in 1991). Assuming that there will be one teacher per class for all the subjects at the primary level, there will be a need for 24,00,000 teachers to teach English from class 1 in 6,00,000 primary classes. The number required will be more if we consider the number of people with professional degrees, who are trained for specific jobs. It will be even more because the primary classes in middle and secondary schools and the multiple sections of a primary class in primary, middle and secondary schools are not reflected in the above figure of the number of primary schools in India. The figure of 6,00,000 primary classes, therefore, is certainly on the low side; single-teacher primary schools will not make the figure to be on the high side. The number of primary class teachers needed by this liberal estimate, who are likely to have the capability to teach English, works out to be 20% of those who know English. It means that one in every 20 persons, who can be considered to have learnt some English, must become teachers in primary schools if English is to be taught from class 1. It is obvious that that many of the English-knowing people will not become primary school teachers. English is not imagined by people as a ticket to a teaching job in primary schools in villages.

Unacceptable result

The following is illustrative of the way English is taught and learnt in an English medium school for poor children run by the Delhi administration in New Delhi, the capital of the country (Anon., pers. comm.). It brings out tellingly how poor the teaching of the English language is in an English medium school. (It is not difficult to imagine the poverty of English in classes teaching other subjects through that medium.)

> In the English language class of class 5, the teacher of ten-year standing reads aloud a story from an English textbook of NCERT and makes many errors in reading, such as 'The girl cried with tears in her ears'. She stops to translate into Hindi after reading a bunch of sentences. Children ask many questions about the story in Hindi and the teacher answers them in Hindi. No English is used except when reading from the textbook. After the reading of the story is over, the teacher helps the children find answers to the questions at the end of the lesson. She explains each question in Hindi and asks the children to find its answer in the lesson. Most of the children possess a used textbook, which is heavily marked with meanings of words and for answers to questions. With the help of these markings, children locate the answer in the lesson and mark it with parentheses. Then they copy down the marked answer in their notebook. They find and copy answers to each question in this way. The teacher then asks the students to memorise the answers and alerts them that some of those questions may be asked in their examination.

Needs of the majority

It is more demanding to teach English to first generation learners in the primary school even for a teacher who has good command of English. These learners do not get any reinforcement of this language in the environment of their home or outside. With the lack of environment and the lack of speaking model in the classroom, it is unrealistic to believe that longer years of instruction in English will give good proficiency in it. To unlearn and correct any wrongly acquired skill is more difficult than learning the skill correctly. When the teachers and students are not equipped to teach and learn English in class 1, there is no pedagogical case to do it. Doing so may contribute to disproportionate educational failure of first generation learners at the primary level itself, when the declared goal is to have universal primary education.

Pedagogical efficiency

Any language educator will agree that there are common language skills applicable to all languages and transferable from one language to another abstractly (Lightbrown and Spada 1993). There is also consensus that lack of good foundation in speaking in a language will hamper the learning of reading and writing skills in that language. It is a fundamental pedagogical principle that teaching takes the learner from the known to the unknown. The student knows how to speak her mother tongue before coming to the school, but this cannot be said about English. It is pedagogically efficient to develop literacy skills in it first, making use of this advantage of the mother tongue. The literacy skills, being commonly applicable in fundamental respects across languages, can be efficiently transferred from the mother tongue to English. The pre-school oracy skills in the mother tongue and the transferability of language skills argue for developing oral skills and introducing literacy skills in the mother tongue as necessary conditions for efficient teaching of the second language English. Laying a good foundation of language skills in the mother tongue is laying a good foundation for teaching English. This pedagogical efficiency principle suggests that teaching of the second language (English) must start after the foundation for language skills is laid in the first language of the student (an Indian language). This means that successful teaching of English requires successful teaching of the mother tongue.

This way of improving pedagogical efficiency calls for finding principles and practices of integrating pedagogically the teaching of the three languages in the Indian school system. The trial of integration must start at teacher training institutions, where language skill development methods for the three languages are taught independent of each other. The teacher trainees are trained in English teaching methods, Hindi teaching methods and Telugu or any other Indian language teaching methods, but not in language teaching methods per se. Language teaching methods are crucially important for the teachers of primary schools, where the same teacher is most likely to teach the first language as well as the second language. She will benefit immensely by training in integrated language teaching. Mother tongue and English need not be in conflict with each other (Tickoo 1996) with regard to curricular time, teaching methods and inherent value. They mutually reinforce each other in all these. Like the grammars of languages in multilingualism converge, the teaching methodologies and learning strategies do converge in a multi-language curriculum, when artificial language boundaries, motivated by non-pedagogical reasons, are not imposed.

Appropriate methodology

English is learnt as a second language in schools in India unlike in China or Japan, where it is learnt as a foreign language. The difference lies, among historical, social and curricular facts, in the fact of the presence or absence of accessibility to and reinforcement of English outside the classroom. English is present, in speech and in print, in the home, in the neighbourhood and in the media in India. Parents, who help in homework, become partners of the teaching process. This is not the case with first generation learners, who make up the substantial majority of students in rural villages and urban slums. This raises the question whether foreign language teaching methods must be integrated with second language teaching methods while teaching English to first generation learners. Methods and materials of teaching English to urban middle class children from homes where English is in the air may not be universally applicable to all learners from different backgrounds.

Another methodological issue arises from the large size of the class and multi-grade teaching in government schools. Second-language teaching methods emphasise the small size of the class and individual learning. When this is not possible in most schools, responsible language pedagogy is not to impart flawed proficiency of language using its preferred methods, but to retool its methods to suit the existing conditions.

If the learning of English has to move from universal preference to universal achievement, then it is essential to have an integration of the teaching of English with the teaching of the mother tongue and to have innovation in methodology appropriate to learners who come from adverse backgrounds. Successful teaching of English will reduce the demand for English medium instruction and for an early start of English instruction, both of which lead to failure in teaching English to students whose parents and grandparents were denied access to this language by sociopolitical factors, and who now want to equalise their opportunities in the newly opening social and economic systems.

Consequence of the failed method

The consequences of teaching English efficiently as a language are enormously beneficial not only to individuals opening up more opportunities for economic, social and spatial mobility for themselves, but also to the society as a whole. It will take the wind of English medium instruction out of the sail of proficiency in English, promoting an education for the majority that is not rote learning, but is critical learning. Release of the creative potential will increase manifold for advancing knowledge. The second benefit will be a change in the structure of Indian multilingualism to make it more equitable. The current structure of multilingualism is imbalanced because of unequal access to the languages of power, more specifically to English. Acquisition of English is through formal instruction alone in India, and this instruction produces uneven results in English proficiency because of the exclusivist, inflexible and uniform teaching of English. The uneven results of learning English maintain the imbalance in multilingualism while giving the appearance and false hope to the unprivileged that they are catching up. People of this section of the society are hence deprived of opportunities in their post-school life because of their poor English language skills, just as they would have been had they lacked the skills altogether.

References

Annamalai, E. 2004. Medium of Power: The Question of English in Education in India. In *Medium of Instruction Policies: Which Agenda? Whose Agenda?*, eds. James W. Tollefson and B.M. Amy Tsui. Mahwah, NJ: Lawrence Erlbaum.

Bhattacharya, S.S. 2002. Languages in India- Their Status and Function. In *Linguistic Landscaping in India with Special Reference to the New States of India*, eds. N.H. Itagi, and S.K. Singh. Mysore: Central Institute of Indian Languages.

Crawford, J. 1995. *Bilingual Education: History, Politics, Theory, and Practice.* 2nd ed. Los Angeles: Bilingual Education Services.

Cummins, J. 1998. Bilingual Education and English Immersion: The Ramirez Report in Theoretical Perspective. In *Annual Editions: Teaching of English as a Second Language 98/99*, eds. I.A. Heath, and C.J. Serrano. Guildford, CT: Dushkin/McGraw Hill.

Lambert, W.E. and G.R. Tucker. 1972. *Bilingual Education of Children: St. Lambert Experiment.* Rowley, MA: Newbury House.

Lightbrown, P.M. and N. Spada. 1993. *How Languages are Learned.* Oxford: Oxford University Press.

NCERT. 1999. *Sixth All India Educational Survey: Main Report.* New Delhi: National Council for Educational Research and Training.

Prabhu, N.S. 1987. *Second Language Pedagogy.* Oxford: Oxford University Press.

Probe Team, The. 1999. *Public Report on Basic Education in India.* New Delhi: Oxford University Press.

Srivastava, A.K., R. Shekher and B.D. Jayaram. 1978. *Language Load.* Mysore: Central Institute of Indian Languages.

Tickoo, M.L. 1996. English in Asian Bilingual Education: From Hatred to Harmony. *Journal of Multilingualism and Multicultural Development* 17(2): 235–240.

10

Mother Language Education and Cognitive Development

V. Prakasam

The term 'mother language' defies precision. This 'defiance' is multidimensional. Dialectal (geolectal), sociolectal and linguistic variations transcend the homogeneity criterion to give us a precise definition of mother language. Terms like first language, native tongue, home language, all face the same problems—*avyapti* and *ativyapti doshas* haunt them.

Ivan Illich's discussion of mother language and vernacular tongue (Pattanayak 1981) is very enlightening, and his ideas make us raise the following questions:

1. Is the institution of language a political weapon—both in its birth and its growth?
2. Is there any economic consideration in the discussion of mother-language and its ability to unify a group of people?

Before we go further let us go over what Illich has said regarding Nebrija's *Grammatica Castellana* (cited in Pattanayak 1981, 5). 'Language has always been the consort of empire and forever shall remain its mate. Together they come into being, together they grow and flower, and together they decline'. Nebrija's grammar 'was written as a tool for conquest abroad and as a weapon to suppress untutored speech at home' (ibid., 7). This brings us face to face with a peculiar distinction—vernacular v. language, which should be differentiated from the distinction between vernacular v. classical language. 'The term mother tongue, from its very first use, instrumentalizes everyday language in the service of an institutional cause' (ibid., 28). 'The vernacular spreads by practical use; it is learnt from people . . . the model for taught colloquial is somebody who does not say what he means, but who recites what others have contrived' (ibid., 36).

This raises the following questions related to those already mentioned:

1. Is the concept of mother tongue an artifact or a natural phenomenon?
2. Is language a general term we use for different speech forms which are mutually intelligible and which are identified as related forms constituting one language?
3. How is the 'distance' between different varieties evaluated as 'dialectal' or 'linguistic'?

Here let us see what Halliday says (1978, 199). 'The concept of language "distance"—the notion of how far apart any pair of languages is said to be—depends partly on linguistic considerations (language as system) and partly on sociolinguistic ones (language as institution). Sociolinguistically, in terms of status and functions, we can recognize a series beginning with the neighbourhood language, through local, regional and national languages, to an international language . . . A person is more likely to attain a high degree of competence in a language orally related to his mother tongue than in one that does not share such affinity.'

In present times, we find people hesitant to use the term mother tongue because actually we are referring to 'child language'—the language the child grows with and socialises or matures with. The following parallel terms are also used (the year in which each term originated is given in brackets):

Patent tongue

- Language ordinarily used/thinking language (Denksprache)
- The Language of the cultural circle (Kulthur Kreisprace 1934)
- Languages of everyday use (Umgangsprache 1951)
- Language of their homes (Hansprache 1961, Pattanayak 1981, 5)

Andre Martinet's definition of mother tongue is leading for our purpose: 'The language which allows one to have the cognizance of the world is the mother tongue' (Ibid., 51).

Pattanayak (1981, 53) reinforces this: 'The primacy (of mother tongue) is established in terms of concept formation, creative thinking and primary socialization . . . (Mother tongue) can be seen either as a super-ordinated language system or as an institution affiliating home languages which are self-sustained entities'. Further, 'if each language has some sort of defining characteristic of the gestalt of a people, then each new language is bound to provide a new or added dimension to one's perception and cognition of reality' (ibid., 56).

These definitions take us to the second half of the title of this presentation. Sperber and Wilson (1986, 38) rightly say that we are all 'engaged in a lifetime's enterprise of deriving information from this common environment and constructing the best possible mental representation of it'. This, we can say is cognition. Cognition depends on our cognitive abilities, which comprise perceptual abilities and inferential abilities and narrow physical environment. The conceptualisation which goes hand in hand with our language learning, different beliefs and different memories together constitute our cognitive environment.

Halliday (1975, 75) uses the term 'mathetic' for the function language performs in 'enabling the child to learn about his social and material environment, serving him in the construction of reality. This function is realized, in the first instance, through the child's *observing, recalling* and *predicting* the objects and events which infringe on his perceptions' (emphasis mine).

We shall now try to define the concepts of cognition, recognition, de-cognition and re-cognition. Cognition is 'the mental process of knowing, learning, and understanding things'. Recognition is 'understanding and acceptance of a fact or situation'. De-cognition is 'non-understanding and non-acceptance of a fact or situation'. Re-cognition is the 'revised process of knowing, learning and understanding things' (Prakasam 1991, 84).

Let us now get into the very 'process' of cognition, which comprises several other sub-processes. *Perception* is 'the awareness of things we have by means of our senses'. The senses perceive bodies and their qualities. On the other hand, *comprehension* is a mental activity which does not need a physical medium. 'The similitude of the object that mind creates within self, which steers intellectual activities, is sufficient for comprehension' (Abelard in IWT).

'Wordings' are capsules, which abridge 'discourses'. This kind of abridgement actually involves two simultaneous processes:

abstraction and *concraction* (Antoine Drestult de Tracy in IWT). Abstraction is a process through which the mind abstracts an element of a synthesis to consider its proper nature alone. While abstracting, we discover the similarities and differences between objects. Thus are formed general ideas. The ability to abstract and to dissect leads us to general propositions which help memory and give precision to the discourse, the general principles tend to become very vague.

The process of concracting helps us form ideas of existing things and abstract from groups of ideas whose model does not exist in nature, and which are nevertheless very useful in making new comparisons and in perceiving relationships with reference to already known ones. Concracting puts together several ideas to form a singular one. For example, the idea of a peach is formed by combining the ideas of its colour, shape, size, taste and ripeness. This is concracting. Extending the qualities of one peach to all peaches, ignoring individual differences is abstracting. Though antonymous, concracting and abstracting go together always, and both are necessary for the formation of ideas.

'Names', here used in a general sense as items of the lexicogrammar of a language, engender 'intellection' and abridge that intellected 'discourse'. When a word is used, it is claimed the mind supplies the complete definition to the abridged terms, which are employed to avoid confusion that a multitude of words may bring. Certain terms do not even need a definition because nature has given us, besides speech, an intelligence sharper than the one we acquire by explanations. For example, the word 'time' is understood by all without the help of any definition though individuals may differ in their views about the essence of time. Definitions are made only to designate the things we name, not to reveal the nature of these things (Pascal in IWT).

The 'discourse' that gets reflected in our language may be 'imagined' or 'conceived'. When we say, 'The earth is round,' we have the 'earth' and 'roundness' as images in our mind, but the 'affirmation' involved in the sentence is what we can conceive of but cannot imagine. So an 'idea' can be defined as what is in our mind, regardless of the manner in which it is 'conceived', i.e., with or without imagination attendant on it (Antoine Arnauld and Pierra Nicole in IWT).

In all generalisation, there is a specific process of thinking involved. A man who wishes to perceive relationships and to make judgements recalls all the facts among which he sees a link, recalls some more facts to make sure the link he has perceived is real and constant and then examines to what extent the link can be generalised. The absence of facts or the absence of a clear link among facts leads us to confusion. This 'confusion' or its lighter form 'haziness', or 'vagueness', takes interesting forms in the context of a public speech or a seminar presentation.

There is another interesting mode of 'conceptualisation'. On the basis of our experience with different languages and cultures we may be able to talk of certain absolute conceptual categories—these are called 'noemes'. On the other hand, a 'seme' is the distinctive feature available to the speaker of a language as a member of a set. A bundle of semes gives us a 'sememe'. Sememes are different from 'pragmemes'. The latter are the minimal units of coder-based signification .

Here I would like to refer to the Buddhist theory of meaning, *apoha*, which gives us a very useful theory of cognition or conceptualisation. 'According to the Buddhists, words deal directly with conceptual images which are purely subjective constructions of the mind, . . . The meaning of a word is a conceptual image whose essence is the negation of all its counter correlates' (Kunjunni Raja 1977; Prakasam 1985). For example, a well is a 'well' because it is not a river, a lake, a sea or a pool. In English, 'catch' is 'catch' because it is not 'hold'. It is interesting to note that we call white, black and brown cows as 'cow' only by the negation of the non-cow. This view anticipates the Saussurean dictum that in language there are only differences, without positive terms. In response to the serious criticism levelled by the realists, Ratnakirti modified the *apoha* theory by saying that the essence of meaning consists in affirmation qualified by the negation of all other things. When we say 'blue lotus' we cognise 'blue' and 'lotus' simultaneously and to the exclusion of lotuses of other colours and blue things which are not lotuses (Prakasam and Abbi 1986).

I use 'recognition' here in the sense of 'lexico-grammaticalisation' of the cognised world. So, we have already noted that words engender intellection. Each lexical item or even a grammatical category is a capsule with abridged discourse in it. When a word is heard, a discourse is comprehended. To that extent there is recognition. But, what happens in a communication gap is the absence of total isomorphy between what is 'recognised' and what is 'cognised'. Most of us cognise goats as black. But when we see white goats we de-cognise and re-cognise them differently and, as a result, the word 'goat' recognises differently. Whenever people want to conceal their real intentions, they use words that do not really 'recognise'. To that extent they 'de-cognise'. That is why we hear people say, 'Come on, call a spade a spade.'

Langacker (1990, 1999) and Gill and Pottier (1992) provide us the following details of cognitive abilities:

1. experiencing outside phenomena through our senses
2. comparison and categorisation
3. concraction and abstraction
4. attention and organisation
5. conceptual reification—grouping a set of identities and manipulating them
6. mental scanning for sequentiality
7. metaphoricisation

Metaphor is deemed essential to cognitive development. Langacker (1999, 172) rightly thinks that 'developmentally . . . the innate abilities are responsible for the emergence of coherent experience, initially in the physical realm. They are subsequently applied in other more abstract domains' (See also, Halliday and Matthiessen 1999.)

Let us take the case of a child who is growing socially and mentally, a fact which also gets reflected in his linguistic growth. Halliday (1975) equates the learning of a language as the learning of a system of meanings. This system of meanings includes also the awareness of the social roles we play. That is how the individual matures both socially and mentally into a personality. 'Language is the medium through which a human being becomes a personality, in consequence of his membership of society and his occupancy of social roles' (Halliday 1978, 15). 'Learning how to mean is what first-language learning is' (ibid., 19). 'All children have access to the meaning potential of the system; but they may differ, because social groups differ, in their interpretation of what the situation demands' (ibid., 27). 'The ability to use language in abstract and indirect contexts of situation is what distinguishes the speech of adults from that of children. Learning language consists in part in learning to free it from the constraints of the immediate environment' (ibid., 29).

Let us now bring in the idea of mother-language education (MLE), which can be construed to refer to both and study through the mother language. The main hunch seems to be that a wholesome cognitive development is likely if education is imparted through the mother language. Notwithstanding the precision or otherwise of the concept, The following are the most important kinds of ability which characterise the mother language in an educational context.

1. saying same things in different ways
2. hesitating and saying nothing very much
3. predicting what the other person is going to say
4. adding new verbal skills—learning new words and meanings while talking and listening

If education is through a non-mother language (second language, foreign language or a national foreign language), the fear is that the cognitive development will not be adequate and not at the right pace at least. It is true that the SL/FL/NFL cannot be learnt as the child language, but it can be learnt as adult language.

The cognitive development gets enriched and diversified if exposed to different languages. At a later stage of life, 'saving' a new concept may not be as natural, but it would not be difficult either. A word like 'cousin' could come to subsume different 'cousins (and cross-cousins) of Andhra Pradesh' or 'cousins of Uttar Pradesh' and can be cognised after a while (Wa Thiong'o 1986).

It is very important to note that 'progress in thought and progress in speech are not parallel. Their two growth curves cross and recross. They may straighten out and run side by side, even merge for a time, but they always diverge again'. (Vygotsky 1962, 33).

All the same we can agree with the director general of UNESCO Koichiro Matsuura's message for the International Mother Language Day on 19 February 2004. 'Mother tongue languages should be favoured in education systems from the earliest age.' But he also added, 'It is widely acknowledged nowadays that teaching in both the mother tongue and official national language helps children to obtain better results and stimulates their cognitive development and capacity to learn'. It is indeed very true that 'in education the experience of language learning is more important than the actual choice of language' (Baldauf and Ingram 2003).

References

Abelard, P. 1992. Intellection. In H.S. Gill and B. Pottier, ed.

Arnauld, A. and P. Nicole. 1992. Ideas. In H.S. Gill and B. Pottier, ed.

Baldauf, R.B., Jr. and D. Ingram. 2003. Language-in-Education Planning. In *International Encyclopedia of Linguistics*, Vol. 2, 2nd Ed. pp. 412–416.

de Tracy, A.D. 1992. The Formation of Ideas. In H.S. Gill and B. Pottier, ed.

Gill, H.S. and B. Pottier, trans. and cod. 1992. *Ideas, Words, and Things*. New Delhi: Orient Longman.

Halliday, M.A.K. 1975. *Learning How to Mean – Exploration in the Development of Language*. London: Elsevier.

_________. 1978. *Language as Social Semiotic – The Social Interpretation of Language and Meaning*. London: Edward Arnold.

Halliday, M.A.K. and C. Matthiessen. 1999. *Construing Experience through Meaning: A Language-based Approach to Cognition*. London: Cassell.

Kunjunni Raja, K. 1977. *Indian Theories of Meaning*. Madras: The Adyar Library.

Langacker, R. W. 1999. *Grammar and Conceptualization*. Berlin: Walter De Gruyter.

________. 1990. *Concept, Image, and Symbol. The Cognitive Basis of Grammar*. Berlin and New York: Mouton de Gruyter.

Martinet, A. 1992. Markedness and Otherness. In H.S. Gill and B. Pottier, ed.

Pascal, B. 1992. On the Mathematical Mind. In H.S. Gill and B. Pottier, ed.

Pattanayak, D. P. 1981. *Multilingualism and Mother Tongue Education: With the Foreword and an Essay by Ivan Illich*. Delhi. Oxford University Press.

Prakasam, V. 1985. *The Linguistic Spectrum*. Patiala: Punjabi University

________. 1991. English as Medium of Instruction: The Problem of Registral Coordination. In *South Asian Language Review 1:1*.

________ and A. Abbi. 1986. *Semantic Theories and Language Teaching*. New Delhi. Allied Publishers.

Sperber, D. and D. Wilson. 1986. *Relevance: Communication and Cognition*. Oxford: Basil Blackwell.

Vygotsky, L.S. 1962. *Thought and Language*. Trans. and ed. E. Hanfmann and G. Vakar, Cambridge, MA: The MLT Press.

Wa Thiong'o, N. 1986. *Decolonising the Mind: The Politics of Language in African Literature*. London: James Currey.

11

Mother Tongue and the Other Tongues: A Plea for Balance and Action

Robert Bellarmine

Underlying beliefs

This paper is based on four beliefs. One, for the economic development of nations, communities, and individuals in the SAARC region, especially the former colonies of Britain, English is crucial. Two, major languages in the region such as Telugu and Tamil (my mother tongue), may not be so endangered or threatened by English as some minor languages like Tulu and Kodagu. However, in some domains such as social intercourse and primary education so crucial for the survival of languages, English is elbowing out mother tongues, both majority and minority languages. Three, this so-called killer language, English, will continue its dominance regionally and globally for about fifty years. And four, for economic, social, cultural purposes, for a well-integrated self and for 'rootedness', which is vital for psychological well being, bilingualism is a necessity in today's world for both individuals and groups. These beliefs, unlike some religious beliefs, have been informed with scholarly studies and projections (Crystal 2000).

Our first need

To survive economically, we need English for another three generations, to go by predictions by economists within and outside India. To preserve what is valuable in our language and culture, to avoid identity crises and the loss of the sense of rootedness, we need our mother tongues, not just for a few generations but forever. Therefore, in the broadest sense, what we seem to need are, in attitudinal terms, a sense of balance and, in action terms, quite a few balancing acts. In specific terms, what do we need to do? The answer to the question is 'Many things.' I illustrate with a real-life anecdote the first of our needs at a level above and beyond the individual's.

When I joined the British Council, Chennai, Tamil Nadu, in 1986, among the papers my predecessor, Dr N. S. Prabhu, kindly passed on to me, I came across a proposal that was about thirty years old at that time. Thanks to Prabhu's respect for history and eye for ideas, although the idea had been rejected by the proponent's bosses, his paper survived. Dr L. A. Hill, English Language Officer in the Chennai office had proposed, extremely radically by the norms of the 1950s, that the British Council, Britain, in effect, should reconsider promoting just English, and start promoting the teaching of English as well as the local languages. With great vision, Hill was pushing for the council achieving its larger goal of building bridges between nations in a post-war spirit by exploiting what is common between their languages, their cultures, and so on, rather than promoting another of the vestiges of colonialism, English.

As a policy proposal, as a document to be studied by highly qualified senior colleagues specialised in ELT and as an explorative instrument, the paper did not include examples. For reviving the proposal and discussing it widely with the Indian operation of the British Council, and to look for feasible measures for concrete action, I needed examples of language-based, non-divisive, common-cause projects. My guess was, and still is, that among other things Hill must have thought of not abandoning the use of the Council's ELT specialists but getting them to focus on the universal features of languages or language as a general human capacity.

Can we make the idea still more concrete by considering the four language skills and what can be universal about them across the individual language or dialectal boundaries? On this approach, it may not be irrelevant here to recall the following to appreciate Hill's idea. Michael West, after his experiments in Dacca in the 1920s (as Professor M. L. Tickoo and Professor P. T. George have taught their CIEFL teacher trainees year after year) found that training in reading English texts had a transfer effect on the ability to read texts in Bengali and the other way round too. To give a recent illustration, language testing specialists such as Charles

Alderson and reading specialists such as Sandy Urquhart hold the view that some aspects of the reading process and the human capacity to read are not language specific. Similarly, the writing skill and the writing process involve sub-skills and language elements that are not language specific.

Had the views of Hill's bosses been appreciated in the British Council in the 1950s, British applied linguists would be coming here to work, not just with teachers of English but also with teachers of Tamil, Telugu, Hindi, and so on. Had that happened, mother tongue teaching in India and the 125 other countries that the British Council has been serving would have benefited from the teaching of English and the research, materials production, testing and management of learning related to it carried out in the UK.

In the process, I am sure the British would have had the opportunities badly needed to appreciate the richness of other languages, literatures and cultures. This would have helped not only that nation in the process of becoming less monochromatic in its colour and culture but also the British Council in achieving its wider objective of improving mutual appreciation of Britain and other nations.

The action point

I suggest that a brief proposal specifying and arguing the case for a shift of focus from *a language*, or English, to *language*, be drafted, first of all, by a group of friends of Britain and the SAARC countries. This can then be discussed with the directors of the local British Council offices and with appropriate bodies of our own governments. The appeal can then be redrafted, signed by friends of the British Council, the local governments' policy-making bodies and opinion makers, and finally sent to the chairman of the British Council and the council's funding body, the Foreign and Commonwealth Office in the UK. It is not clear to me at this stage which is a better idea: to route it through our own governments or through the local British Council offices.

The second need

The answer to this question comes from my discussions with two influential Tamils, active in the mass media. Mr Annamalai works for the BBC World both as a relationship manager and a professional assistant for programmers in the Tamil Osai division of the BBC Radio. He is also a reviewer of Tamil Internet work, a specialist in Tamil folk literature, and a playwright. Fr Vincent Chinnadurai is the director of Santhome Communication Centre in Chennai, which produces dance, drama, and music programmes for the radio and television. He is also a well-known Tamil writer. Formerly, he was secretary of the Minority Commission of the Tamil Nadu government. While Mr Annamalai studied in Tamil Nadu, Fr Vincent studied in the US as well as in Tamil Nadu. Further, while Mr Annamalai's education was by and large through the medium of Tamil, Fr Vincent's was through English. However, both have continued to study Tamil literature and publish mostly in Tamil.

One of the questions I posed to them was, 'What role has your Tamil teachers played in the development of your love for your mother tongue and your literary and critical writing skills in your mother tongue?'. His Tamil teachers' influence on Mr Annamalai was, in his words: 'Minimal, almost nothing!' On the contrary, Fr Vincent's teachers, two of them, one at the school and the other at the college level, had played an extremely significant role. Where the two interviewees agreed was in the strong adherence to the view that the teaching of Tamil, and in fact, of all our mother tongues, should be improved in schools.

The two persons had been trained in pedagogy, and they proposed the following with regard to the teaching of Tamil.

- The texts prescribed from post-primary levels onwards should have fewer number of ancient and classical texts in order to ensure an increase in content relevance and appropriateness and also in the modern forms of the language.
- The classroom pedagogy should be interactive and experiential.
- The texts should include more contemporary literature and dialect studies.
- The excessive focus on classical Tamil and literature can be reduced by increasing the room for language for practical, occupational, academic, business, scientific and technological purposes.
- In other words, to save our mother tongues, some of our actions need to be internal with no reference to English or other dominant languages.

The third need: economic indicators

Another need is to make education policy makers, curriculum designers and classroom teachers concerned with our mother tongues and English sensitive to the general tendency today to evaluate things predominantly in economic terms. When we send a project proposal these days for funds, whether it is an educational project or a project for women's empowerment or for AIDS education, we need to do almost always a sociological, technological, economic and political (STEP) analysis. What we in language education or language planning have not successfully done yet is to develop formulas, procedures and guidelines for assessing the value of language education or language proficiency in economic terms.

Put differently, we have not yet been able to monetise language education or language matters. Britain has estimated its annual income from selling its English-related goods and services in pound sterling terms. These estimates are mainly based on physical objects such as books, CDs and cassettes that are tangible and directly purchasable, along with specialists' fees and salaries. On the other hand, suppose a politician or a bureaucrat sincerely asked applied linguists, language planners, language educators or educated parents, 'What are the commercial or economic benefits of developing the survival level of proficiency in English or Spanish or Chinese, in rupee or yen or Singapore or US dollar terms?'. The honest answer would be, 'We don't know!'

In 1994, for the Dunford House Conference in the UK, the British Council and applied linguists in British universities were supposed to study the issue of assessing the benefits of English language projects in monetary terms. This was required by the Overseas Development Administration (ODA), now called the Department of Foreign and International Development (DFID), as Britain's largest aid funds provider for the British Council and for India.

Before the seminar, the head of English Studies, at the British Council in Delhi, Dr Neil Gilroy-Scott, consulted all his English Studies officers in India as well as Indian specialist institutes, located in Delhi and Bangalore, that dealt with such matters. I am sure his counterparts did the same in the council's other offices in Africa, Europe and the rest of Asia. However, the proceedings of the 1994 Dunford House Seminar said honestly and candidly that despite the desperate need, the specialists at the seminar were unable to arrive at even an approach to evaluating the monetary value of language matters.

What is the difficulty?

My own theory is that, unlike economists of the remote past and specialists of the recent past, we in higher education in general and language education in particular are obsessed with an absolute sense of accuracy. We seem to lack the confidence and an attitude of certainty that one needs to initiate the difficult process of arriving at an equation assigning concrete monetary values and numbers to what is relatively intangible, namely, language and the benefits of language.

Economists know that no currency or monetary system is one hundred per cent standardised or standardisable with a zero-error margin. There is nothing like an absolute, universal standard even in monetary matters. One US dollar in the US does not have the same purchasing power as it has in Portugal or in India. This is why economists have now come up with the idea of purchasing power parity (PPP), to be used across economic zones worldwide. In other words, accuracy of formulas and procedures and equations in economics evolved and are still evolving. When the need to move from the barter system was felt, a crude form of money was invented.

We in the language profession have perhaps reached that stage now. The need now is to confidently produce a formula or a set of guidelines to assess the monetary value of proficiencies in our mother tongues as opposed to that in other tongues; the monetary value of business presentations in our mother tongues as opposed to that in other tongues; and AIDS education campaigns in our mother tongues as opposed to other tongues, and so on.

Recommendations

I propose that we adopt a two-stage action plan. First let a study group of specialists in applied linguistics, economics and education arrive at procedures for calculating the economic benefits of language activities; and second, let a small but influential group meet political leaders, business leaders and bureaucrats for studying the scope for using the formulas in education, business and overseas aid.

References

Crystal, D. 2000. *Language Death*. Cambridge: Cambridge University Press.

Section II

Critical Classroom Practices

12

Postmodern Epistemology and Causality: Research Theory and Application at the Crossroads

Dale Thomas Griffee

In the 1980s and 1990s, the discussion of evaluation concentrated on the type of data being collected. If quantitative data or numbers were collected, the evaluator was considered hard, positivistic, factual, scientific and she or he probably used large standardised tests. If qualitative data or words were collected, the evaluator was likely to be considered soft, naturalistic, interpretative, and also that he/she probably liked narrative storytelling. Today this division based on types of data is being abandoned, and evaluators find an opening to rethink the rationale for classroom evaluation at not only the data collection and analysis level, but also at the level of basic philosophical orientation.

The thesis of this paper is that we are in the midst of a change in the underlying theory of educational evaluation from one termed as the standard view to one not yet agreed on. This change in philosophical orientation is important because of implications for classroom evaluation and teaching. This paper argues that the new orientation is postpositivism using a realist model of causality. It is specifically aimed at classroom teachers interested in evaluating their classes who face the issue of causality in two common circumstances. One is when they try an innovation in their class, measure results and conclude that the innovation was responsible for the improvement. Another is when they try a new way of presenting and assessing a programme of some sort (writing in my case) and would like to understand how the new way works by constructing a causal chain of events to explain it.

Definitions

The following are brief definitions of terms that appear in this paper. Also given is an outline of the model used.

- Philosophical orientation: general assumptions teachers have towards the world and their teaching, often held at an implicit level of understanding
- Causality model: a more specific epistemological theory of how evaluators judge that one event is linked to another event
- Research design: the way an evaluation is conceived and organised in terms of what type of data is collected
- Data collection: the type of data that is sought for the design
- Quantitative data: data in numbers
- Qualitative data: data in words
- Data analysis: how the data is to be analysed and interpreted
- Validity: the process of accumulating and explaining evidence that the analysis interpretation is warranted

The model used in the paper has three parts: philosophical orientation, theory and application. The philosophical orientations discussed are positivism and postpositivism. The theory consists of specific philosophical contexts termed the standard view and a realist understanding, and approach discussed in terms of variable and process, and causality models described as Humean regularity and critical realist. The application part of the model consists of a favoured or preferred design which is experimental and case-data collection described as quantitative and qualitative, and data analysis and validity in terms of inferential statistics and the search for a causal mechanism.

Philosophical orientation: positivism and postpositivism

The philosophical orientation dominant in the first half of the 20th century was termed positivism which contains the view that all theoretical terms must be definable in terms of observation (Phillips 1990, 33). At the core of positivism was the verifiability theory which held that for a proposition to be meaningful, it has to be potentially verifiable, that is, shown to be either true or false. The theory was used to dismiss metaphysics, religion and ethics (Mulaik and James 1995, 119).

In its broadest sense, positivism is a rejection of metaphysics. It is a position that holds that the goal of knowledge is to describe the phenomena that we experience. The purpose of science is simply to stick to what we can observe and measure (Trochim 1999, 27). Trochim cites the behaviorists whose mantra was study only what we can observe. Since we cannot observe emotions, they are not legitimate topics for scientific study. The world and the universe were deterministic to the point of being mechanical and operated by laws of cause and effect. The features of positivism include

(a) the belief that science is largely a mechanistic affair;
(b) deductive reasoning is used to postulate theories that can be tested;
(c) based on the results, theories are revised;
(d) observation and measurement are the core of scientific endeavour;
(e) experiment is the key design; and
(f) meaningful discussion is possible only about what can be observed and verified.

What happened to positivism? Positivism was rejected by the majority of scientists in the decade immediately following World War II because it was shown to be untenable (Mulaik and James 1995, 119; Phillips 1990, 33). What made it untenable was that some scientists were talking in a meaningful way about some very small things they could not actually see, namely, subatomic particles, while other scientists were talking about some very large things they could not see and verify, namely, black holes. What could replace positivism? After the fall of positivism, the term postmodern has been used in a broad sense to refer to any philosophical orientation seeking to replace positivism. Thomas Kuhn's *The Structure of Scientific Revolutions* introduced the word 'paradigm', a term that has since become popular to describe new philosophical orientations. Gage (1989), for example, suggests three such paradigms: objective-quantitative, interpretive-qualitative and critical-theoretical. Guba (1990) offers postpositivism, critical theory and constructionism, and House

(1991) suggests interpretivism, pragmatism and critical theory. This paper argues that of the many possible orientations, postpositivism offers the best support for research because it can accommodate other postmodern paradigms including the ones listed above.

Postpositivism is generally not well understood. For example, Guba (1990) argues that postpositivism is essentially the same as positivism, and Rea-Dickins and Germaine (1998) lump all researchers who use quantitative data as positivists. They write, 'For some time there has been a debate between positivists who view objective empirical methodology as generating measurement-driven data for evaluation and constructivists who deem that appropriate and often ethnographic methodologies are to be used according to the demand of the context and its participants' (ibid., 18). This is positivism by association; researchers who use measurement-driven data for evaluation are positivists. Their logic is as follows:

(a) Bank robbers want money.
(b) You want money.
(c) Therefore, you must be a bank robber.

But just as it is possible to want money and not be a bank robber, it is also possible to use measurement-driven evaluation and not be a positivist. What is postpositivism? Postpositivism is, in fact, a wholesale rejection of the central tenets of positivism (Phillips and Burbules 2000, 4; Trochim 1999, 27.

Postpositivism argues that context is important. Wittgenstein, for example, argues that meaning includes not only the reference (existence) of objects, but also the manner and place (context) of the utterance. Remember that the preferred research design for positivism was the experiment which considers context noise to be eliminated or controlled. Experience is not all there is. Popper and others argue that theoretical propositions cannot be determined to be true or false on the basis of experience alone (Mulaik and James 1995, 121). There is no direct connection between consequences (data) and a hypothesis (theory). Postpositivists argue that in any research, the consequence could be true, but the hypothesis false because there could be other reasons for consequences to be true. Or, the consequence could be false, but the hypothesis true because various auxiliary theories which support the hypothesis could be true or false.

Observation is theory laden. Wittgenstein used the duck-rabbit figure to illustrate fundamental ambiguity in interpreting experience. Hanson (1958) argues that what we see is what we are taught to see, and our observations reflect the theories we accept. He argues that observation is theory laden (Phillips 1990, 34).

The empirical underdetermination of theory

The positivists believed that inductive reasoning is the gathering of data, and from that data a unique theory could be derived (Mulaik and James 1995, 124). But this has been challenged. Current views include the ambiguity of inductive reasoning which can be summed up in the statement 'More than one curve may be constructed to pass through a given set of points.' The major implication of the underdetermination or non-uniqueness of generalisation from particulars of experience is that experience alone is not sufficient to account for our knowledge (ibid.). A variety of rival theories or hypotheses can always be constructed that are equally compatible with whatever finite body of evidence is currently available (Phillips 1990, 35). We can never be certain that the theory we have accepted is the correct one.

The implication is that the acquisition and justification of knowledge is regarded as a social process (Mulaik and James 1995, 125). Postpositivists accept the notion of social construction of reality (Phillips 1990, 43). In fact, Trochim (1999, 28) believes most postpositivists are constructivists, who believe that each of us constructs our view of the world based on our perceptions of it. Postpositivists accept the notion of objectivity, which is a regulative ideal that underlies all enquiry. If we abandon such notions, it is not sensible to make enquiries at all. If a sloppy study is as acceptable as a careful one, why enquire at all? We might just as well accept any view we desire. We need to take pains to be as precise and unbiased as possible (Phillips 1990, 43).

Objectivity of an enquiry does not guarantee its truth; in fact, nothing can guarantee that we have reached the truth. Phillips (ibid.) gives the analogy of two firms that make radios: one is careful and gives a good warranty and the other is sloppy and does not provide a warranty. Either firm may produce a faulty radio, but one is better off with the good firm and the warranty.

Specific philosophical context: standard view and realism

According to Maxwell (2004), the standard view is the Humean regularity model of causality, with events explained by general laws. According to House (1991), the standard view is that facts are foundational, theories are deductive, causality is Humean regularity and, it could be added, that experimental research design with pre-test, post-test control group and experimental group is preferred as the only design considered capable of establishing causality.

What is realist philosophy? In this paper, I argue that realist philosophy is the best possible replacement for the standard view. House (ibid.) gives six characteristics of critical realism:

- There is no foundation such as facts.
- Knowledge is social and historical; facts are theory laden.
- The world is complex and stratified (Bhaskar, 1979).
- Reality is composed of experiences, events and structures.
- Experiences are empirical, actual and real; events are actual and real, but not empirical.
- Structures are real, but not empirical or actual. For example, let us imagine a teacher in a classroom with students. At the experience level there are a multitude of empirical sense impressions including the sights, sounds and feelings of various participants. The positivists would stop here and say that empirical experience is all there is. Realists would continue by saying the event is the course, and the structure the concept of education. They reject the Humean or regularity ideas of causality.

Scientific explanation is not subsumed under laws: it is an explanation of how structures produce events. Explanation is more important than description. The guiding metaphors are mechanism and structures. A naive realist would look at a lemon and say that it is really yellow. A critical realist would say that lemons tend to appear yellow because of the nature of light waves (mechanism) and the structure of the human eye.

Approach: variance theory and process theory

What is variance theory? A variable is any finding that can change or vary (Vogt 1999). Variables can be measured, for example vocabulary scores on a certain test or grade point averages. Variance theory deals with variables (Maxwell 2004) and is closely associated with the standard view, experimental design and statistical analysis. Process theory, in contrast, deals with events and the processes that connect them; it is based on the analysis of causal processes by which some events influence others (ibid. 5).

Causality models: the regularity model and the realist model

I have briefly discussed postpositivism which I would nominate as a replacement for positivism. Now, I will discuss another area of concern, namely, a model of causality. I believe this is an important issue. For many researchers, the model of causality used is assumed and implicit rather than clearly defined, but the causality model used by evaluators guides research by influencing the kind of questions the researcher asks, the type of evidence the researcher will look for and accept, and the type of explanation they will provide.

The regularity model

The regularity model was articulated by David Hume and elaborated by J. S. Mill. Positivism ruled out the possible existence of any entities not directly empirically verifiable through experience. This stance, known as the verification theory, was abandoned, but the regularity model of causality survived. Hume argued that we cannot actually see causality, only its effects which appear between events. Hume's classical example was a billiard ball on a billiard table approaching another billiard ball, hitting it, stopping, and the second billiard ball continuing. In other words, causality is a black box (ibid. 2004). We can observe input to the black box and outputs from the black box, and we can ask ourselves if there is a systematic relationship between them. If there is, we can infer causality. Causality is not inferred by a single case, but only by establishing a pattern. The regularity requires a comparison and is closely associated with experimental design and inferential statistics. Maxwell (2004) suggests evaluators can pose at least three research questions:

1. What is happening? (description)
2. Is there a systematic effect between variables? (causality)

3. Why is it happening? (mechanism)

Maxwell says that experiments using the regularity model might be able to answer questions (2) and (3), but in practice are more comfortable with question (2). For example, Carver (1978), in discussing causality and the validity of confirming a research hypothesis, maintains that researchers need (a) careful design (to set up a comparison and collect data), (b) multiple replications of the findings (because one instance would not be enough), and (c) rigorous theorising (to establish causality).

The realist model

Humans can act intentionally, which enables them to act on the world, monitor their performance, and monitor the monitoring. This last second-order monitoring is called evaluation. Researchers ask what the constructs are that make these actions and meanings possible. Social relationships are open, so experimental research is difficult. As a result, social sciences are explanatory rather than predictive. It is possible to predict some social events, but these predictions lack the certainty, precision and stability of the physical sciences. Laws in an open system are revealed as tendencies (House 1991, 6).

A realist conception of causation sees events as being produced by the interaction of a multitude of underlying causal entities operating at different levels (ibid. 7). This does not mean that causes cannot be determined in specific situations. The realist conception of causation would call for evaluation approaches that describe programmes and their outcomes so that influences can be registered and causal entities and their interactions can be understood. One might draw inferences from experiments, with the help of substantive knowledge, but one would not expect the studies to yield critical tests of the programme (ibid. 8). House, Mathison and McTaggart (1989, 14) cite Searle (1983) for intentional causation. I drank because I was thirsty. I need no further observation, I know the effect and the cause of my action. I don't need any universal law to tell me that cause and effect are logically related, and in this case I can experience the causality. What I experience is my intention of wanting and doing the act. We do not need a covering law to explain things, rather the causal nexus is internal to the experience itself.

This does not mean that experimental design is entirely wrong or useless because rigorous designs may be useful in some situations (House, Mathison and McTaggart 1989, 15).

The complaint that critical realism has against the regularity model is that the latter strips context away and looks only at variables. The realist model sees the causal mechanism in its context. Interestingly though, Maxwell (2004) claims that the realist model can accommodate both experimental and correlation research design as well as single-case design.

Practical application: research design, data collection and data analysis

Deciding on a research design is the first step in moving from theory to practice. Research design presupposes a model of causality as well as epistemological theory, and for this reason, design selection is the most theoretical aspect of practical application. Research design can be viewed as the blueprint for a research project. Just as there are types of houses one can build or buy, there are types of research designs one can employ. A design specifies, among other things, data collection and analysis. The design most closely associated with the standard view is called experimental, and I would argue, the design most closely associated with a realist perspective is the case.

What is experimental design? Classroom teachers seldom use pure experimental design, instead opting for a variation called quasi-experimental design (Cook and Campbell, 1979; Shadish, Cook and Campbell 2002). Both typically employ a pre-test to establish the pre-existing situation and a post-test to show what happened in the end. Statistical analysis is typically employed to compare post-test results between the two groups (see Griffee 2004). The standard view uses variance theory, a regularity model of causality, and prefers some form of experimental design. The idea is (this is explained by Griffee himself) to identify and isolate a variable, design an instrument to measure it, validate the instrument in a pilot study, apply the variable to one group, but not to the other, and then compare results. If the experimental group scores higher, causality is inferred and justified by showing statistical significance.

In terms of the three research questions Maxwell (2004) mentioned in discussing causality, an experimental design is good at answering the question whether there is a systematic effect between variables. It has more trouble providing the mechanism and thus answering why it happened. There are problems with any experimental design, and these problems can be discussed in terms of validation.

The role of validity in experimental design

In using an experimental design, it is necessary to state as clearly as possible what we are doing, and then provide some evidence that we did it. This process of offering evidence that we are doing what we claim to be doing is called validation (for a discussion, see Brown 1988; 1996).

There are three areas in experimental design that require validation: (a) the instruments used to gather data, (b) the argument for causality (called internal validity), and (c) generalising the conclusions to other situations (called external validity). What is case design? One design closely associated with realist process theory is case study; however, though there is currently much discussion on research design, no consensus has had time to form. Case study design is the mirror image of experimental design because case design is helpful when what you are studying is so context embedded that it is hard to distinguish, isolate and measure variables (Yin 1993). The more control one has, the more possible that some form of experimental design can be used, and the less control one has, the more possible a case design can be used (Cohen, Manion and Morrison, 2000; Creswell 2003). A case can be one person, an entire class of students or a whole school. The case is what the evaluator will study, not a general problem or theme (Stake 1995, 1998). Yin (2000) defines case study as having three aspects: data from multiple sources, a real-life context, and theory if results are to be generalised. Case design has great appeal to classroom teachers because we seldom have randomised assignments, enough students for both a control class and an experimental class, and often our work is highly contextualised. In my basic writing classes, despite a high mortality rate, I was able to use an experimental design to establish that a brain-based interactional writing curriculum based on

Smilkstein (2003) produces better results than the traditional lecture-based curriculum. My conclusion on three traditional measurements was that the brain-based interactional curriculum was so superior that I could not in good conscience replicate my findings with another experiment using a control group and my traditional lecture format. As a result, I am using a case study to examine what happens because even authorities such as Cook and Campbell (1979) recommend a case-study design to assess whether there was a treatment and how well it was delivered.

There is a current debate on whether a case study can reveal causality. Some, for example Cohen, Manion and Morrison (2000), say it can while others, for example Cook and Campbell (1979), say it cannot. Researchers operating out of a realist model maintain that it can, because the mechanism for causality can be found in the context which is precisely what case study considers, whereas experiments do not (House 1991; Pawson and Tilley 1997).

The role of validity in case design

Historically, there has not been much concern for validity by those attracted to case design and other types of interpretive studies because their subjective stance does not require a validation process (Greene 1998). The world, however, is not generally willing to accept research and evaluation reports on face value. As a result, those in what Green (ibid.) calls qualitative research do, in fact, seek to show that they are reporting valid empirical reports rather than biased subjective reports by using such validation measures as triangulation, member checks, negative evidence and peer debriefs (Hitchcock and Hughes 1995).

Conclusion

In terms of teacher education, I would expect at least two trends to increase as teachers adopt a postpositivist-process point of view. One is that more teachers will attempt their own classroom research and evaluation. It would be a mistake, however, to assume that research under postpositivist philosophy will be easier than under the positivist approach. Instruments will still require validation. And, I suspect, experimental research design and inferential statistics will continue to be used. A second trend will be an increase in case design using a realist model of causality. Classroom teachers will find mechanisms and structures that directly affect their classroom and pedagogy, and this finding will be exciting and will perhaps provide the motivation to engage in the hard work that research under any philosophical orientation requires.

References

Bhaskar, R. 1979. *The Possibility of Naturalism: A Philosophical Critique of the Contemporary Human Sciences*. 3rd ed. New York: Routledge.

Brown, J.D. 1988. *Understanding Research in Second Language Learning*. Cambridge: Cambridge University Press.

________. 1996. *Testing in Language Programs*. Upper Saddle River, NJ: Prentice Hall Regents.

Carver, R.P. 1978. The Case Against Statistical Significance Testing. *Harvard Educational Review* 48 (3): 378–399.

Cohen, L., L. Manion and K. Morrison. 2000. *Research Methods in Education*. 5th ed. London: Routledge.

Cook, T.D. and D.T. Campbell. 1979. *Quasi-experimentation: Design and Analysis Issues for Field Settings*. Boston: Houghton Mifflin.

Creswell, J.W. 2003. *Research Design*. 2nd ed. Thousand Oaks, CA: Sage Publications.

Gage, N.L. 1989. The Paradigm Wars and Their Aftermath: A Historical Sketch of Research on Teaching Since 1989. *Educational Researcher* 18 (7): 4–10.

Greene, J.C. 1998. Qualitative Program Evaluation: Practice and Promise. In *Collecting and Interpreting Qualitative Materials*, eds. N.K. Denzin and Y.S. Lincoln Thousand Oaks, CA: Sage Publications.

Griffee, D.T. 2004. Research in Practice: Understanding Significance Testing Program Evaluation. In N.K. Denzin and Y.S. Lincoln, eds. *Journal of Developmental Education* 27 (3): 28–34.

Guba, E. C. 1990. The Alternative Paradigm Dialog. In *The Paradigm Dialogue,* ed. E. G. Guba. Newbury Park, CA: Sage Publications.

Hanson, N. 1958. *Patterns of Discovery*. Cambridge: Cambridge University Press.

Hitchcock, G., and D. Hughes. 1995. *Research and the Teacher: A Qualitative Introduction to School-based Research*. 2nd ed. New York: Routledge.

House, E.R. 1991. Realism in Research. *Educational Researcher* 20 (6): 2–9.

________, S. Mathison and R. McTaggart. 1989. Validity and Teacher Inference. *Educational Researcher* 18 (7): 11–26.

Kuhn, T.S. 1970. *The Structure of Scientific Revolutions*. 2nd ed. Chicago: University of Chicago Press.

Maxwell, J. A. 2004. Causal Explanation, Qualitative Research, and Scientific Inquiry in Education. *Educational Researcher* 33 (2): 3–11.

Mulaik, S.A. and L.R. James. 1995. Objectivity and Reasoning in Science and Structural Equation Modeling. In *Structural Equation Paradigm Dialog*, ed. R. H. Hoyle. Newbury Park, CA: Sage Publications.

Pawson, R., and N. Tilley. 1997. *Realistic Evaluation*. Newbury Park, CA: Sage Publications.

Phillips, D.C. 1990. Postpositivist Science: Myths and Realities. In *The Paradigm Dialog*, ed. E.G. Guba. Newbury Park, CA: Sage Publications.

Phillips, D.C. and N.C. Burbules. 2000. *Postpositivism and Educational Research*. New York: Rowman and Littlefield.

Rea-Dickins, P., K. Germaine. 1998. The Price of Everything and the Value of Nothing: Trends in Language Programme Evaluation. In *Managing Evaluation and Innovation in Language Teaching: Building Bridges,* eds. P. Rea-Dickins and K. Germaine. London: Longman.

Searle, J.R. 1983. *Intentionality*. Cambridge: Cambridge University Press.

Shadish, W. R., T.D. Cook, and D.T. Campbell. 2002. *Experimental and Quasi Experimental Designs for Generalized Causal Inference*. Boston: Houghton Mifflin.

Smilkstein, R. 2003. *We are Born to Learn: Using the Brain's Natural Learning Process to Create Today's Curriculum*. Thousand Oaks, CA: Corwin Press.

Stake, R. E. 1995. *The Art of Case Study Research*. Thousand Oaks, CA: Sage.

________. 1998. Case Studies. In *Strategies of Qualitative Inquiry*, eds. N. K. Denzin and Y. S. Lincoln, Thousand Oaks, CA: Sage.

Trochim, W. 1999. *The Research Methods Knowledge Base.* 2nd ed. Cornell University, Ithaca, New York: Cornell Custom Publishing.

Vogt, W. P. 1999. *Dictionary of Statistics and Methodology*. 2nd ed. Thousand Oaks, CA: Sage Publications.

Yin, R. K. 1993. *Applications of Case Study Research*. Newbury Park: CA: Sage Publications.

________. 2000. Case Study Evaluations: A Decade of Progress? In *Evaluation Models: Viewpoints on Educational and Human Services Evaluation* 2nd ed., eds. D.L. Stufflebeam, G. F. Madaus and T. Kellaghan. Boston: Kluwer.

13

Implementing Writing Across the Curriculum (WAC) in Hong Kong

George Stanley Braine

My introduction to Writing across the Curriculum (WAC) came at the University of Texas at Austin when, in the mid 1980s, I was searching for a topic for my doctoral research. My interest was writing in engineering and science, and I wanted to do an ESP-type needs analysis. I discovered that Texas had a well-established WAC programme which required undergraduates to take two writing-intensive courses in their respective disciplines in order to graduate. For my research, I focused on WAC courses in the faculties of engineering and the natural sciences, collecting a wealth of data on the writing in these two areas and also learning much about WAC (Braine 1989; 1995).

During my research, I observed biologists, physicists and engineers using writing creatively in their courses and inspiring their students to become critical thinkers and better writers. To my surprise, some of the papers written by students in these courses were as good as those written by English majors. I began to realise that the teaching of writing could be extended beyond the English department, and that teachers across the disciplines could serve as teachers of writing and as models of good writers. Later, when I taught at the University of South Alabama, I again came to know the WAC programme at that university quite well and became convinced of its effectiveness.

The year after I arrived in Hong Kong, I applied for a Teaching Development Grant sponsored by the University Grants Commission (UGC) to fund the WAC programme. I was turned down. But a proposal I submitted in 2002 jointly with Professors Carmel Mc-

Naught and Joanna Williams of the Chinese University of Hong Kong (CUHK), and which also included professors Ken Hyland of the City University of Hong Kong and Sima Sengupta of the Hong Kong Polytechnic University as cosupervisors, was funded at HK$4 million. This enabled us to launch the WAC programme in September 2002.

What is WAC?

Writing Across the Curriculum (WAC) is an acronym that became popular about three decades ago in the United States to denote attempts by some tertiary institutions to extend student writing beyond the English departments. Although these programmes are initiated by English departments, academic departments from across the university have input into their implementation (Young and Fulwiler 1986).

Central to the ideology of WAC is the question 'Who owns writing?'. Because effective writing is fundamental in tertiary education, responsibility for writing should be vested in the disciplines where writing takes place and with the teachers who are the ultimate authorities over what is considered effective writing in their respective disciplines. As such, WAC has played an important role in emphasising the importance of writing in all disciplines, beyond its traditional home in English, rhetoric and composition departments.

Why should teachers from all disciplines encourage writing in their courses? The reason is that writing is intimately connected with two fundamental processes that teachers attempt to instil in their students—thinking and communicating. Requiring students to write about the content of academic courses is a way of getting them to think about the contents in an active manner, instead of passive memorising or textbook underlining. Active, critical thinking requires higher-level intellectual skills such as the understanding of concepts, the analysis of information, the evaluation of evidence, and the construction and testing of hypotheses. If teachers want students to think about the content of their course, the students should be given the opportunity to write, and thinking will be hard to avoid (see Fulwiler & Young 1990 for reports on WAC programmes in the United States which show that they develop students' critical thinking and communication skills).

What is critical in the Hong Kong context is that this ability to communicate specialised knowledge effectively to an audience needs to be developed in the students' second language, English. Hong Kong students need to have more writing practice than their native speaker counterparts in the United States, but at present they have less. At the CUHK, we hope to redress that imbalance through the Writing across the Curriculum programme.

Rationale for WAC in Hong Kong

Even before the handover to China in 1997, there were perennial complaints about the English proficiency of university students in Hong Kong (Bolton 2002). Seven years after the handover, there is growing pressure from the Hong Kong community to see the enhancement of English proficiency among university students. WAC programmes would be useful at Hong Kong universities because the short 3-year-degree plan leaves most students with little opportunity to take writing courses offered by English departments and English centres. By incorporating writing in English into courses in their majors, students will enhance their English proficiency while improving their thinking and reasoning skills. Interdisciplinary cooperation will occur, and teachers across the disciplines will further benefit through the creation of a community of scholars committed to the improvement of teaching and learning.

English language proficiency, at the level of sophistication worthy of tertiary education, is vital for Hong Kong's global competitiveness. Among the language skills, writing is ranked highest in terms of cognitive complexity and presents difficulty even to native speakers. As stated earlier, educators in the United States have recognised the intimate connection between writing and higher cognitive skills of critical thinking and effective communication, and have established WAC programmes at many colleges and universities. The WAC programme in Hong Kong has been implemented following the procedure and model of well-established WAC programmes in the United States.

In Hong Kong, research has shown that writing in English is the most important language skill for academic success. Hence, the WAC programme will have a significant impact on the university because of the drive to improve the English proficiency and critical thinking skills of students. Under the 3-year curriculum, some CUHK students may graduate from the university without taking any writing courses, any English courses, or for that matter, any courses taught in English. Thus, to enhance the students' writing skills and English proficiency, a significant amount of writing can be introduced to existing courses in other disciplines.

The place of process writing in WAC

In essence, WAC aims to promote more writing across the curriculum. If a course does not include writing assignments, we hope that at least one writing assignment could be included. If a course requires only a term paper (to be submitted at the end of the semester), we hope that a proposal could be required halfway through the semester, so that students could reflect and plan the term paper better. If a course requires only the final version of a paper, we hope that a draft could be required, so that students could receive feedback on their writing and revise it for an improved final paper. We also hope that peer reviews of papers could be introduced to courses across the curriculum. Reflective writing, without the pressure for a grade, is another possibility.

The backbone of the WAC programme is the process approach to writing. Until well into the 1960s, the focus of writing instruction in the United States was the correction and grading of students' papers,[1] with the emphasis being placed on writing style. The composing process was entirely the students' responsibility: 'The assignment went in at one end, and out came the final paper at the other' (Bizzell 1986, 50). However, with more and more underprepared students entering tertiary education, students began to show more than stylistic deficiencies, and organisational, grammatical and mechanical errors also became prevalent. Teachers began to realise that instead of grading the finished product, they would have to intervene in the writing process. Accordingly, the process approach to writing instruction, which includes prewriting exer-

---

[1]As Ilona Leki (2003, 109), coeditor of the *Journal of Second Language Writing,* stated so succinctly, during her 'college years [in the United States] professors didn't give feedback; they gave grades, and there were no second drafts, no peer commentary. It just wasn't done, didn't exist'.

cises, journal writing, peer reviews, multiple drafts of papers, and teacher–student conferences, began to be used in writing instruction. According to Fulwiler and Young (1990, 2), who coordinated a pioneering WAC programme at Michigan Tech, one of the goals of the WAC movement is to promote 'process-oriented composition pedagogy'.

Although the process approach has been advocated by Hong Kong's Department of Education since 1994, research indicates that due to various constraints, the process approach is not utilised in Hong Kong secondary schools (Braine 2003). At the tertiary level, at least in courses conducted by English departments and English centres, the evidence suggests that the process approach is being used. But to extend it to courses across the curriculum is a challenge.

Objectives of the WAC programme in Hong Kong

In the grant proposal, we outlined the objectives as follows:

- identify undergraduate courses that could be included in a WAC programme;
- conduct mini-workshops for teachers from the university;
- conduct workshops for teaching assistants;
- assist teachers to incorporate writing in their courses;
- establish a University Writing Committee consisting of teachers of various disciplines and chaired by cosupervisors of this project; and
- provide a model of implementation for the further expansion and dissemination of WAC programmes in Hong Kong.

The Hong Kong WAC model

Because the concept of WAC in higher education is American, we had to make certain adaptations for Hong Kong. First, in the United States, although WAC is generally housed in English departments (mainly because that is where the writing specialists are), the teaching assistants (TAs) or tutors who actually interact with students are not from English departments. For example, a course in biology affiliated with the WAC programme may have a TA who is a graduate student in biology, who, in addition to his/her tutoring duties, would also provide feedback on students' writing assignments, having been trained by the WAC programme. These TAs, as undergraduates, would have taken one or more writing courses, where the process approach to writing would have been practised. Many of them also have the advantage of being native speakers of English.

In Hong Kong, the attitude to writing among local (Cantonese) non-English department professors is starkly different. Considering that they had the option of teaching in Cantonese, it is admirable that some professors have chosen to teach in English. However, as I have shown elsewhere (Braine 2002), having received little or no writing instruction during their secondary school and undergraduate studies in Hong Kong, they do not require their students to write much. Further, TAs affiliated to various courses (who themselves are graduate students), unlike their counterparts in the USA, may not have taken any writing courses as undergraduates, and, in any case, may be mediocre writers. Hence, instead of training TAs from across the curriculum, the WAC programme provided the TAs.

A second adaptation was the decision to affiliate graduate courses as well. The American model focuses on undergraduates, on the assumption that the WAC courses are extensions to required first-year courses in writing (the so-called freshman writing courses). However, early in our programme, we received requests to work with graduate students as well, especially as they wrote their MA theses in the summer months. From the current academic year, we are affiliated to a few graduate courses as well, on the assumption that we would be most effective where we are invited to participate.

A third innovation was the writing mini-workshops, often designed and always conducted by the TAs. Early in our programme, some professors saw the need to provide their students information about process writing, plagiarism, etc. Because our TAs had higher

Table 1 *Differences between the US and Hong Kong WAC programmes*

USA	Hong Kong
TAs are subject specialists employed by academic departments	TAs are applied linguists employed by the WAC programme
undergraduate courses	undergraduate and postgraduate courses
mini-workshops rare	mini-workshops frequent

degrees in applied linguistics and had a grounding in second language writing, we decided to become proactive and conduct mini-workshops, which, for the most part, have been well received.

Implementing WAC

Our first task, upon the award of the grant, was to recruit teaching assistants. We chose MPhil degree holders in applied linguistics, especially those who had taken a postgraduate course titled 'Second Language Writing', which I teach. We conducted a workshop for the TAs on providing feedback on writing. Then we sent out invitations to all the professors in six of the seven faculties of the Chinese University (see Appendix A). We did not include the faculty of medicine because our budget would not allow us to support the largest faculty of the CUHK.

The response was not overwhelming. Two professors questioned how writing generalists could respond to discipline-specific writing. So we reached out to professors we knew personally, explained our objectives and persuaded them to join the programme. We did make some mistakes in the first semester and stumbled into courses where our resources were wasted. Some courses that were affiliated to the WAC programme did not include any writing assignments, and others had only one term paper due at the end of term.

In the first semester of 2002–2003, seventeen professors from the CUHK were affiliated with the project. They taught a total of twenty-one courses and represented sixteen academic departments. One workshop was conducted for the professors (see Appendix B for the agenda) and more workshops for the TAs were also conducted. We held weekly project meetings, and weekly reports were submitted by the TAs (see Appendix C for sample weekly report). We also created a website (www.cuhk.edu.hk/wac) and published a newsletter which was distributed to all non-medical teachers of the Chinese University and selected staff at the City University of Hong Kong.

As the semester progressed, a few professors requested that the TAs conduct mini-workshops for their students on various aspects of writing. So we designed a number of 30- to 60-minute mini-workshops based on power point, with titles such as 'How to be a better writer', 'Plagiarism: What it is and how to avoid it', 'The writing process: 8 steps', 'Writing a scientific report', 'Conjunctions', 'Making an effective oral presentation', and 'Process writing'. By the end of the semester, 15 mini-workshops were offered to students. The TAs had also provided feedback on 440 papers written by students and conducted 239 one-to-one writing conferences with students. Their performance was evaluated by the professors to whose courses the TAs were affiliated.

In the second semester of 2002–2003, seventeen professors from the CUHK were affiliated with the project. They taught a total of twenty-one courses and represented sixteen academic departments. We also extended the programme to the City University of Hong Kong and Hong Kong Polytechnic University. At the City University, two professors teaching three courses were affiliated with the project. At the Polytechnic University, four professors teaching five courses were affiliated. We continued to hold weekly project meetings and the TAs wrote weekly reports. We also designed additional mini-workshops titled 'Effective professional presentations', 'Using connectives', 'Tenses', 'Writing a proposal in manufacturing engineering', 'Writing and delivering a speech', 'Writing a venture-idea proposal', 'Writing a field trip report', 'Writing literature reviews in quality management', 'Academic writing skills for human resource management students', 'Annotated bibliography writing tips', and 'Abstract writing tips'. In all, thirty-four of these mini-workshops were conducted. During the semester, the TAs provided feedback on 1,329 papers and conducted 363 one-to-one writing conferences with students. As in the first semester, the TAs' performance was evaluated by the professors.

A university writing committee, which would monitor the WAC programme and also act in an advisory capacity, was formed. In addition to the project supervisors, the committee consisted of professors from journalism, systems engineering, sports science, and the English Language Unit. The second newsletter was be issued and distributed to all non-medical teachers of the CUHK and selected staff at the City University and Polytechnic University. A workshop titled 'How to enrich your courses with writing assignments' was conducted.

At the beginning of our second year, we took a long and hard look at the programme. When we began the programme, we extended an open invitation to professors to be affiliated with WAC. We later conducted two workshops on process writing for professors and also described the principles of process writing in our newsletters. However, we realised that some professors still required only end-of-term papers, with no requirements for drafts and thereby no allowance for feedback. Hence, from the second year, we became more selective and decided not to affiliate TAs to some courses. With Professor Ken Hyland leaving the City University, we decided not to return there. We also realised that the culture of Polytechnic University was quite different and decided not to return to that institution. However we affiliated one course from HK Baptist University at the request of the professor concerned. During our second year of operation (2003–2004), our TAs provided feedback on 1,059 papers and conducted 499 one-to-one conferences with students. They also led 67 workshops (see Table 3).

Table 2 *WAC affiliations from 2002–2003, 2003–2004*

	2002–2003 Semester 1	**2002–2003 Semester 2**	**2003–2004 Semester 1**	**2003–2004 Semester 2**
Professors	17	23	19	25
Courses	21	29	26	31
Academic departments	16	16	15	20

Table 3 *Workload handled by WAC teaching assistants, 2003–2004*

2003–2004	**Students enrolled**	**Feedback on papers**	**One-to-one conferences**	**Mini-workshops**
Term 1	821	545	209	44
Term 2	801	514	290	23

Overall, up to the end of its second year, the WAC programme had been affiliated with 81 courses taught at the Chinese University of Hong Kong, the City University, and Polytechnic University. Of the 300 English medium courses taught at the CUHK, WAC has already been affiliated with 73 courses, some for more than one term. A total of 2,413 students have benefited directly from the WAC programme.

Evaluation of the WAC programme

The most effective evaluation would be the examination of students' writing before and after they have been enrolled in a WAC course. We do not have the human resources for such a study but hope it would form the basis for an MPhil or PhD study.

At a more fundamental level, the WAC programme's effectiveness could be judged on the basis of the amount and types of writing in courses before and after they were affiliated with WAC. Textual and anecdotal evidence suggests that this is occurring. A scrutiny of course syllabi shows that reflective writing is practised, proposals are being written, multiple drafts are encouraged, and peer reviews are being conducted. In one course, students are rewarded with extra points for good writing. Anecdotal evidence, in the form of interviews with a few professors (for the WAC newsletters), also indicates that both the quantity and quality of writing has seen an improvement. We are now designing an error analysis of students' writing to examine the effects of the TAs' feedback as well as a holistic evaluation of students' papers (as in the Teaching of Writing in English, or TWE) before and after the TAs' intervention.

However, research that I conducted at the University of Texas at Austin and the University of South Alabama (see Braine and Bradford 1993) indicates that professors are prone to emphasise the quantity of writing more than the process approach. Of the 51 WAC courses examined, only 26 used at least one process-oriented technique. This indicates that in Hong Kong, where most professors are non-native speakers of English and writing receives less emphasis in courses, the adoption of WAC practices may be a long time in coming.

At the end of each semester, the professors evaluate the TAs who are affiliated to their courses. Decisions on course affiliations for subsequent semesters and contract renewals for the TAs are made on the basis of these evaluations. More recently, students have also been encouraged to provide feedback on the TAs performance, especially their conduct of mini-workshops.

Long-term objectives

The WAC programme has been funded for three years, till the end of the 2004–2005 academic year. On the basis of WAC models in the USA, our long-term plans are as follows:

- At least one course in every academic department at the CUHK is to be identified as a WAC course. This could be based on the quantity of writing required in the course, and/or the number of writing assignments required and the adoption of the process approach to writing. The latter would be defined as the writing of a proposal midway through the semester for an end-of-semester term paper—with the requirement to submit a draft before the final version of a paper is written; the use of peer reviews; and the encouragement of ungraded reflective writing.
- In order to graduate from the CUHK, all undergraduates must have successfully completed at least one WAC-affiliated course, preferably in the students' major.

Appendix A: Invitation letter to professors

September 7, 2002

Professor . . .
Department of History
CUHK

Dear . . .,

I am writing to invite you to participate in the newly established Writing Across the Curriculum (WAC) programme at the CUHK. The goal of the WAC programme is to improve the English proficiency of CUHK students in all disciplines by enhancing their writing skills. As an integral part of the curriculum in the United States, WAC programmes have proven effective in developing students' skills in writing and critical thinking.

A team from the CUHK has been awarded a Teaching Development Grant for 2002–2005 to pioneer this model in Hong Kong. Our team consists of Professor George Braine from the English department as principal supervisor and Professor Joanna Radwanska-Williams from the English department and Professor Carmel McNaught from CLEAR as co-supervisors. Our staff includes several full-time teaching assistants, who all hold postgraduate degrees in applied English linguistics.

We would be delighted if you would participate in the WAC programme because you teach undergraduate course(s) in English. Through workshops hosted by CLEAR, the WAC programme will enable the sharing of ideas about teaching methodology among faculty members across disciplines. Starting in September, the teaching assistants will be assigned to selected courses to help you to provide feedback on students' written assignments. Later this semester, we will invite interested colleagues from all departments to participate in a WAC workshop.

At this initial stage, could you indicate your willingness to participate in the WAC programme by completing and returning the attached reply slip? An addressed envelope has been enclosed for your convenience. Thank you for your response.

Sincerely,

George Braine
Associate Professor and Principal Supervisor, WAC

Appendix B: Agenda of a workshop for professors

How to Enrich Your Courses with Writing Assignments

WAC@CUHK

Tuesday, 5 August 2003
10.00 a.m.–12.00 p.m.
FHK Room 125

Facilitators: George Braine, Joanna Radwanska-Williams, Carmel McNaught

WELCOME

1. Introductions for all participants, including the nature of any existing writing component in courses

2. What is WAC?

3. Process writing

4. Writing assignments—designing the proposal, organising drafts, etc.

BREAK

5. Handling a peer review
(Exercise based on an example. Participants to work in pairs.)

6. Feedback from group about applicability and viability of these ideas

7. Workshop evaluation

Appendix C: Sample weekly report submitted by a TA

Paulina Cheung Weekly Report November 11–15, 2002

I considered the consultation with Hau Ka Sing rewarding. Hau is a first-year History student. I remember vividly that he wrote poorly in his first History essay. That was totally disorganized, and without references. He got C- for his essay and I was kind of worried about this student. He showed real improvements after consulting with me four times. His last essay was a B+. This morning, he asked me what aspects he could further improve. I told him to avoid the use of personal pronouns in academic writing. He said to me that I was really helping him in the development of his writing skills. He said he would praise me highly in the course evaluation.

I faced a difficult challenge in the History class too. A student named Wong Ho Ming loved writing long, complex sentences, with fancy words. I encouraged him thousands of times to write short sentences with approximately 15 words per sentence. He always talked back and argued that the ELTU staff told him to write with around 25 words per sentence. He believed that one of the features of academic writing was the use of complex sentences. However, when I read his paper, he did not demonstrate good examples of complex sentences. In other words, he seldom used nominalization. His long sentences mostly consisted of verbs and prepositions. Many times, his essays showed a clear signs of Chinglish. I felt very frustrated. I almost lost my voice after his consultation. He was stubborn most of the time. Don't know how to help him. Prof. Potter noticed this and she had talked to this student individually.

Also, I felt very frustrated after talking to Prof. Y's Teaching Assistant. I asked him to encourage the students to submit their first drafts. Here were his responses in the e-mail: 'I won't encourage the students to submit the reports now since the deadline is already come. Moreover, the less students submit, the less reports we need to correct, ha ha!'. I was responsible for the language aspect. He was required to read the content as Prof. Y told him to. I remember Dr. Braine not long ago wrote an article entitled 'When Professors don't cooperate'. Perhaps I can write an article called 'When Teaching Assistants don't cooperate'. In the end, twenty-nine articles were collected. My colleague Derek did the first reading, and I did the second reading. Having marked the reports, in three hours' time, I tabulated and analyzed students' common errors in their report writing. Please see the attached 'Top Thirteen problems in PHY2001 students' Report Writing'. The attachment served as an overall comments on the students' report writing. Prof. Y and the students will all get a copy of it.

So much for this week. I was totally exhausted.

References

Bizzell, P. 1986. Composing Processes: An Overview. In *The Teaching of Writing*, eds. E.R. Petrosky and D. Bartholomae. Chicago: The National Society for the Study of Education.

Bolton, K. 2002. Introduction. In *Hong Kong English: Autonomy and Creativity*, ed. K. Bolton. Hong Kong: Hong Kong University Press.

Braine, G. 1989. Writing in Science and Technology: An Analysis of Assignments from Ten Undergraduate Courses. *English for Specific Purposes Journal* 8: 3–15.

_______. 1995. Writing in the Natural Sciences and Engineering. In *Academic Writing in a Second Language: Essays on Research and Pedagogy*, eds. D. Belcher and G. Braine NJ: Ablex.

_______. 2002. When Professors Don't Cooperate: A Critical Perspective on EAP Research. In *English for Specific Purposes* 20: 293–303.

_______. 2003. From a Teacher-centered to a Student-centered Approach. *Journal of Asian Pacific Communication* 13: 267–286.

_______. and Bradford, L. 1993. Writing across the Curriculum: A Study of Faculty Practices at Two Universities. *Issues in Writing* 5: 157–186.

Fulwiler, T. and A. Young. 1990. *Programs that Work*. Portsmouth, New Hampshire: Boynton/Cook.

Leki, I. 2003. Tangled Webs: Complexities of Professional Writing. In *Writing for Scholarly Publication*, eds. C.P. Casanave and S. Vandrick. Mahwah, N J: Lawrence Erlbaum.

Young, A. and T. Fulwiler. 1986. *Writing across the Disciplines: Research into Practice.* Upper Montclair, N J: Boynton/Cook.

14

Adults Becoming Bilinguals and Becoming Teachers

Greta J. Gorsuch

Ten years ago, I interviewed a young Japanese high school teacher of English in a rural high school outside Tokyo. He described the moment when he first began to teach, using English as the medium of instruction: 'The students were surprised. I could see surprise on their faces, and they started shouting, "I don't know what he's saying!" At that time, I was afraid that I couldn't use English freely, so my voice was tense and maybe my face was red. I felt extremely tense' (Gorsuch 1993). As one of only two high school English-using teachers out of a total of eighteen English teachers at the school, Mr Kaneko's decision to use English in class was quite a statement. In Japan, high school teachers spend a great deal of time together, crammed into one large teachers room, at least five days a week from, seven-thirty in the morning until five in the afternoon. No doubt, word spread fast about Mr Kaneko's use of English. As the school was one that specialised in preparing young Japanese for form-focused university entrance exams, Mr Kaneko's use of English was marked. With a good deal of content to get through in each lesson, what would be the point of using English to explain it, which would be a waste of time? In other words, how could he reconcile the primary requirement of his job (cramming students with nuanced grammar points for exams) with his belief that students should use English? At the very least, Mr Kaneko's decision to use English was fraught with implications for his career.

Yet Mr Kaneko reported being satisfied with his decision. He believed that his use of English helped him become a gentler, more sympathetic teacher. He said that he became highly aware of changes in his English use and his pedagogy. As he became better at managing the classroom in English, he found that his skill in explaining grammar in English, and also bilingually, improved. He began to repeat points more frequently and became better at monitoring students' comprehension of content by using daily evaluation forms which students would complete. If one accepts Snow's (1993, 392) definition of bilinguals as people 'who actually function . . . in more than one language', I would argue that Mr Kaneko became bilingual through his use of his second language to teach. He did not use English outside school and thus functioned in his second language only in his role as a teacher.

I would like to extend our discussion on bilinguals and bilingual education to adults who become teachers in their second language and in some cases, I would argue, become bilingual through their use of English as teachers. Through my descriptions of such adults, I hope to highlight the opportunities and challenges that such people face. I will draw connections between choices adults make concerning the use of their second language in specific contexts when they function as teachers and the implications of their choices on a personal level, on their language development, on their teaching, and on the societies and education systems in which they work and act.

Two groups

I describe here two groups of adult bilinguals I have worked with. One group is Japanese high school teachers of English using English in their classrooms with Japanese students, and the other group is international teaching assistants enrolled as graduate students and teaching classes in their fields of study to freshmen college students in the United States. In both cases, these teachers and apprentice teachers are using English as their second language in classroom settings, and this fact will colour the comments I make. English is an influential language in the international scene, and this undoubtedly has altered the decisions of many of the adults I have worked with (see Valdez 1998). If, for example, Hindi were a dominant language spoken throughout the world for purposes of commerce and education, many of the young Indian Hindi-speaking scholars I work with would not have made the decision to seek a graduate degree in the US and to become apprentice teachers in classrooms in which they must use a second language to succeed.

Japanese teachers of English in Japan

Japanese teachers of English in Japanese high schools number in tens of thousands. My work has been with 876 teachers at academic and vocational, public and private high schools in nine rural and urban prefectures. Their teaching experience ranged from one to thirty years. Foreign language education in Japan would be termed by Siegel (2003, 179) as an 'external L2' context, in which foreign languages are viewed as a 'foreign or distant language' and are learned by speakers of a single dominant language, such as Japanese. For both cultural and philosphical reasons, Japanese educational authorities have traditionally conceived of English as a body of content and a means by which to compare Japanese culture with the cultures of English-speaking countries (Law 1995). To learn English as a foreign language in high schools means translating difficult English texts into Japanese and then discussing the grammar points and usage in Japanese. In such classrooms, teachers have little reason to use English (Gorsuch 1998). Form-focused, translation-based university entrance exams which generally contain a large section on English, strongly influence high school foreign language instruction and mitigate against acceptance of communicative activities in the classroom (Gorsuch 2000). Japanese high schools are ranked according to the rank of the universities that the students pass entrance exams for, and teachers are rewarded for high acceptance rates of students into better universities (ibid.). Since using Japanese is seen as the most efficient way to transmit content in the form of grammar instruction, teachers are not rewarded professionally for 'wasting time' in class by using English or asking students to participate in communicative tasks.

For political reasons, there have been some official moves towards increasing the societal expectation that English be taught as a means of communication. In 1987, Minoru Wada of the Ministry of Education managed to enact the Japanese English Teaching (JET) programme, which called for a limited number of Japanese teachers of English to team teach with native English-speaking assistant language teachers (ALTs). The intent of the programme was to have Japanese teachers and ALTs interact in English and to raise Japanese teachers' awareness of English as a communicative medium (Wada and Cominos 1994). As one of the boldest national language-teacher education programmes known in the world, the JET programme employs more than five thousand ALTs and has a budget of over 200,000,000 US dollars. It has been reported that Japanese teachers have requested to work with an ALT, but conflicting reports suggest that ALTs have been foisted on Japanese teachers by overzealous prefectural education officials. However, whether Japanese high school English teachers came into contact with ALTs, I argue that it is as a result of programmes like JET and similar programmes adopted by private high schools in Japan that a new group of Japanese adults who became bilingual as they functioned as teachers has emerged. There is both quantitative and qualitative evidence for this. In a large-scale survey study, I found that of the 876 high school English teachers, 179 reported teaching with an ALT at least once a week. The latter group of teachers differed in several important ways from teachers who had little or no contact with ALTs.

Japanese teachers of English (JTEs) who reported teaching with ALTs at least once a week had a statistically significant higher self-rating of their ability to use English in class. JTEs who reported teaching with ALTs less than once a week or not at all rated their classroom English ability lower. JTEs with extensive contact with ALTs agreed less that they had studied English through traditional grammar-translation methods (*yakudoku*) than JTEs with limited or no ALT contact. JTEs who team-taught with ALTs at least once a week reported being more approving of a communicative information-gap activity than JTEs who had limited or no ALT contact. This difference was statistically significant.

The Japanese teachers' decision to interact and work with ALTs has had implications for their self-perceptions of their language ability and even the extent to which they identify with the traditional teaching method (translation) prevalent in Japan. As a further consequence, their perceptions of what constitutes appropriate pedagogy have changed. There is also qualitative evidence for an emerging group of bilinguals. Yukawa (1994) did a year-long case study of in- and out-of-class interactions between a Japanese high school English teacher and an ALT. She found that over the course of a year, the Japanese teacher's in-class utterances became more frequent, longer and more complex to the point where nearly the entire class was being managed in English.

The implications of Japanese high school English teachers' decisions to function as bilinguals in the classroom go beyond their personal and professional lives. As Japanese teachers use more communicative English in classrooms and ask their students to communicate, they are in effect changing their goals and, thus, their curricula. In the best of worlds, Japanese high school English teachers will become an emerging voice for a broad scale reconceptualisation of the purpose of English and other second languages, from the classical view of the grammar of a language as an academic subject to a social utility or a multicultural view which encourages direct engagement with the languages and cultures of other countries (Ornstein and Hunkins 1993). As active and visible users of English, Japanese teachers serve as role models to high school students, who may shift their own self perceptions of what they wish to accomplish in learning a second language.

International teaching assistants in the United States

The second group of adult bilinguals I work with are international teaching assistants (ITAs) who have come to the United States to attend graduate school. ITAs at my school are international students from twenty or more countries who seek graduate degrees in disciplines such as physics, chemistry, biology, economics and political science. As is typical of graduate students in American universities, they are expected to teach basic undergraduate classes in their disciplines. This is done partly to apprentice them as future teachers in their fields, partly to financially support them in their study, and partly to provide cheap teaching labour. At any given point, there are over 400 ITAs working at my university, and I come into contact with approximately 120 of them per year, either through my official capacity as a language assessor or as the director of an ITA education programme which offers courses throughout the academic year. To even describe them as a group is difficult, but I provide here some descriptive information taken from a group of sixty-six ITAs who recently attended a three-week summer workshop at the university.

They were studying in seventeen different disciplines: seventeen ITAs were in chemistry, eight in linguistics, four in Spanish, four in German, four were in mathematics and the rest in political science, mechanical engineering, economics, French, marketing, biology, computer science, physics, family studies, hospitality and statistics. They represented twenty nationalities with twenty Chinese, ten Indian, six Korean and six Turkish. The rest were German, Japanese, Tunisian, Mexican, Bangladeshi, Brazilian, Cambodian, Cameroonian, Chilean, French, Israeli, Romanian, Russian, Spanish, Sri Lankan, Uzbekistani and Vietnamese. Thirty-eight in the group were men, and twenty-eight were women. Their mean age was 28 years, with the minimum being 21 and the maximum being 51. Thirty-eight of the sixty-six were newly arrived in the US, with the rest having an average stay in the country of nine and a half months. Twenty-six of the ITAs had been students in the US previously. There were ten Chinese, four Turkish, two Korean and two Indian ITAs as well as one each from Bangladesh, France, Mexico, Germany, Israel, Cambodia, Chile and Sri Lanka. Only nine of the sixty-six ITAs had ever taught in the US before. Two were from India, and the rest came from Bangladesh, Russia, France, Mexico, Israel, Korea and Turkey. Thirty-one of the sixty-six had never before taught in their home countries. As we can see from this information, ITAs are highly individualistic in their backgrounds. Theories on international education and teacher development suggests real diversity in the educational experiences individuals have which operate above and below the level of the country of origin (Cohen and Spillane 1992, Davis 1991, Freeman and Richards 1993, Gorsuch 2003, Holliday 1994, Lortie 1975, Wang, Martin and Martin 2002). Yet two basic groups seem to have emerged within the ITA population at my school: one group that has learned English in an 'external L2' context, and another group that has learned English in an 'institutional L2' context (Siegel 2003). These differences have implications for whether or not ITAs are functionally bilingual when they first arrive, and for the kinds of choices they must make after their arrival. ITAs from 'external L2' contexts have learned English as a 'foreign or distant' language in countries that view English language as an academic subject to be learned for cultural reasons. These ITAs are from Chile, China, Korea, Japan, Mexico, Romania, Spain and Vietnam. While being educated or working in the professional or academic world in their home countries, ITAs in this group must make extraordinary efforts to become functionally bilingual for social, business or educational purposes. They must seek out opportunities to use English in contexts where such opportunities may be limited. To become bilingual must be a matter of conscious choice. English is unlikely to be used as the language of instruction at either the high school or college level, so ITAs from such contexts have not heard English being used to manage information or to realise pedagogy in a classroom setting.

Many ITAs coming from an 'external L2' language context are not functionally bilingual upon arrival but then over time become so as teachers, and possibly socially as well. ITAs from such contexts often do not have sufficient control over grammar and lack adequate vocabulary range to communicate in classroom and even social settings. When placed in classrooms, many ITAs struggle with procedural and relational language necessary for conducting labs and for explaining content to American undergraduates. They also struggle with the appropriate register to use with students and with recognising and solving communication breakdowns.

In order to understand the kinds of choices about language that 'external L2' ITAs must make after arrival, it is necessary to understand the situation awaiting them. It is unlikely that ITAs choose to come to the US because they wish to teach; what attracts them is the education and, possibly, the entrance into an international life. But from the point of view of the academic departments in the university, ITAs must teach like all other native English-speaking TAs in order to participate in what the university perceives as normal graduate-level educational processes. There are strong incentives for ITAs to teach. Three departments hiring the largest number of ITAs (chemistry, physics and biology) have adopted policies requiring ITAs to become eligible to teach within one year if their support is to be continued. To become eligible to teach, ITAs must pass a series of assessments stipulated by the Texas Education Code. While the assessments are valid and fair, passing them is easier said than done, and ITAs from 'external L2' contexts must make some fairly hard choices in order to deal with them. On a personal level, even while they are attending graduate content courses in their second language on a full-time basis, they must find ways to learn the language they need to function as teachers. They need to be resourceful as, strangely, American university settings do not provide many opportunities for ITAs to learn to teach in English. As students, most ITAs focus on content rather than on the linguistic forms their teachers use to manage information. Further, most universities do not provide non-teaching, low-language-level ITAs access to freshman courses to observe and practise teaching.

There may also be social and cultural impediments to learning English. If an ITA comes from a first-language group that is already well represented at the university, it may be difficult for the ITA to disassociate himself or herself from the group and make friends with those who do not share his/her L1. As an example, Mandarin L1 Chinese make up the majority of ITAs in any given workshop or class offered in the ITA training programme at my university. From self-reports that ITAs from all L1 groups complete, most Chinese ITAs say that aside from attending classes in English at the university and reading the required study matenals in English, they use Mandarin for home life, socialising and doing research. To pool resources, they share apartments, cars and funds. In the words of one Chinese ITA, 'If I use English all the time, I should move out, because I have a Chinese roommate.' ITAs whose L1 groups are not well represented at the university may find it easier to choose having meaningful social contacts among English L1 speakers.

Many ITAs from 'external L2' contexts choose to take ESL courses at their own expense, which means they do not have as much money, time or energy to devote to their graduate studies or families. Other ITAs choose to immerse themselves in self-study, and devote time to 'beating the test'. They seek out test materials, which are furiously circulated within the ITA's L1 community, as are textbooks. Some succeed using these methods and become teachers in their departments in six months to a year. How they are as teachers, and whether their language development continues after this point is beyond the scope of this paper, but the topic definitely deserves investigation. Some ITAs choose to leave this struggle and find employment as research assistants, which allows them to remain at a very basic level of bilingualism. Others choose to leave after a year.

I have identified one group of ITAs who come from an 'external L2' context for descriptive purposes, but I would like to stress that individuals within this group differ greatly in the kinds of choices they make that influence their language development and their development as teachers. I would like to describe choices made by two ITAs from this group to illustrate more clearly the connections between their choices and their growth as teachers using a second language. Both ITAs participated in a practicum course at my university in which ITAs struggling with language issues are paired with experienced TAs and ITAs. The ITAs are expected to attend their host TA's class once a week, observe and gradually increase their involvement in the class to the point where they can conduct a lab, answer students' questions and conduct part of a lecture. Such practices are likely to provide focused opportunities for ITAs to attend to linguistic input, to engage in negotiation of meaning with native English speakers, and to engage in pushed output.

May (a pseudonym) is a Chinese biology doctoral student, who is married and has a young daughter. Before her daughter began attending an American school, May was the only English speaker in her household. She attended the practicum for one semester and was paired with an American TA in an honors lab, but felt she did not progress as much as she would like. During an observation of one of the labs, May could be seen circulating around the room, working hard to interact with students but somehow not succeeding in sustaining any one conversation. The next semester, May chose to try the practicum again but this time requested that she choose the hosting TA. It happened that she went to several TAs and queried them on the content to be covered in their labs and on the degree to which they would agree to allow her to teach and have some authority in the classroom. May believed that she needed to work in a setting more aligned with her own research interests in the area of cell biology. She also believed that she needed to have more responsibility of the kind that would force her to speak. May found a TA who suited her needs and then requested her department to allow her to be a 'prep specialist' for the lab. They agreed. That semester, due in large part to May's choices and active intervention in her own language development, May made real progress. Two observations of the lab revealed her as an active participant in continuous, sustained conversations with both the students and the TA. She offered to teach, and was largely successful at it. She passed the state-required assessments a few months later and, at the time of writing this, is teaching her own biology lab.

Minh (another pseudonym), is a Vietnamese economics doctoral student. He is single and is one of the three Vietnamese students at the university. He attended the practicum for one semester in a lecture style course taught by a Pakistani ITA with highly superior language and teaching skills. In most required economics classes, American undergraduates are silent and passive, but the experienced TA skillfully cajoled the students into discussion by persistently using phrases such as 'I haven't heard anything from that side of the room. Does this mean you understand everything?' In interviews, Minh said repeatedly that he wanted to become an effective teacher and get students to discuss and think for themselves. By all appearances, the hosting ITA's class was perfect for Minh to take a practicum in. But in multiple observations of the class, Minh remained entirely passive, sitting in the back of the room. On several occasions the hosting ITA invited Minh to answer the students' questions or conduct review sessions, but Minh would smile and shake his head. On the one occasion when Minh was scheduled to teach a class, he backed out at the last minute, claiming illness. Over the course of the practicum, Minh made consistent decisions not to use English in teaching settings. It may be argued that a lecture-based course offers fewer opportunities than labs for low-language-level ITAs to interact with American students and engage in the kinds of tasks known to develop language and teaching skills. But it is precisely in this kind of situation that ITAs' choices take on great significance. ITAs who choose to actively pursue every opportunity to engage in teaching tasks in their second language may succeed in becoming teachers at the university, while those ITAs who choose a passive role may not. As it turned out, Minh did not pass the teaching assessment that semester, and at the time of writing this paper, still does not teach.

While both May and Minh are members of their respective departments, I would argue that by being a teacher, May operates at a higher level of involvement in her department, in a manner which is highly approved of. At a societal and educational level, her American students, most of whom are from small towns in Texas, benefit from interacting with a non-American student whose knowledge and views are very different. If May elects to return to China as an academic, she will stand out as someone who can teach in a valued second language, and will be in a position to influence future generations of Chinese biologists to perhaps gravitate towards living and working abroad. Minh may not be able to continue in his department if he cannot either find a research assistantship or take up again the challenge of developing his language and teaching abilities.

The second group of ITAs I will report on are ITAs who have learned English in an 'institutional L2' context. These are ITAs who, as students, have learned and used the second language English as an 'imported language with a wide range of official uses,' most probably as students (Siegel 2003, 179). These ITAs are from countries like Bangladesh, Cameroon, India, Pakistan, Sri Lanka and Turkey. In contrast to ITAs from 'external L2' contexts, who report knowing only their native language and English, ITAs from 'institutional L2' contexts appear to be able to operate as multilinguals in multilingual environments. They report not only knowing several languages (for example Marathi, Hindi and English or French, English, and Nganya), but using at least two of them on a regular basis. They also report speaking at least two languages for ten or more years, which, given their mean age of 28 years, account for a good part of their lives. ITAs from 'external L2' contexts report that though they had learned English for only five or six years, they started speaking English only a week or two before the survey conducted to collect this data.

Having been educated in English, ITAs from 'institutional L2' contexts are functionally bilingual at a social and academic level. To the extent to which they are apprentice teachers through their roles as students in a second language environment, they have some familiarity with English or another second language used to manage information and direct classroom activity. ITAs in this group have a different set of challenges to face and choices to make upon their arrival at the university. As with 'external L2' ITAs, it is necessary to understand the context 'institutional L2' ITAs operate in, which constrains their choices. Because they are functionally bilingual upon arrival, and possess a wide range of academic vocabulary and good control over many grammatical forms, many 'institutional L2' ITAs pass the state assessments quickly, and are just as quickly assigned to teach labs and classes. Some departments are impressed with these ITAs' language skills as compared to the skills of ITAs from 'external L2' contexts and so do not send them to be assessed. In either case, however, this means that the ITAs are not eligible for courses designed to help them with English pronunciation or other aspects of second language use. This is significant in that many 'institutional L2' ITAs have serious problems with North American English suprasegmental pronunciation, such as word stress and sentence and discoursal emphasis. They know a lot of academic terminology, but have used it in their home countries using very different patterns of word stress, which often impedes their comprehension of North American English speakers. It is often difficult to know which points in their discourse the ITAs wish to emphasise, resulting in what sounds like endless and undifferentiated sentences. If one transcribes a lesson given by an ITA from this group, it is clear that the person is expressing complex concepts and the relationships between them in quite sophisticated ways, and yet because they do not emphasise the key markers of the concepts or the relational language used to order them, the same message in spoken form is indeed very difficult to follow. It is not always the case that 'institutional L2' ITAs are aware of the problems they are having with pronunciation. As full-fledged teachers and graduate students, it is expected they will focus on the work before them, and thus they do not have access to ESL professionals or others who could draw their attention to specific pronunciation issues. Colleagues or supervisors may comment on their pronunciation, and if they have serious problems, they are most likely to learn about them through student evaluations. The standardised student evaluation form which my university uses does not address language issues, and while students may write in a comment that they cannot understand their TA, they probably would not know how to describe specific problems they have with comprehension. Poor student evaluations may preclude ITAs from benefiting from the good opinion of faculty members, who recommend ITAs for monetary teaching awards, scholarships, coveted internships and jobs.

ITAs from this group are quite aware of one other language issue, and this has to do with cultural referents that American students, colleagues and faculty use in everyday speech (sociolinguistic competence). ITAs from 'institutional L2' contexts frequently report that while they are aware they are missing pieces of information in speech they hear around them, they cannot parse out what is being said. Even when they can hear the actual words, they do not know what the words refer to. ITAs in this group admit being frustrated by this, as in their self-reports, they state, 'I wish to know how Americans speak,' and 'I wish to be able to communicate better with English speakers.' From other remarks they have made, it seems that using English effectively with English speakers in the US is connected to becoming an international person: 'If I learn to use English very well, I think I will easily integrate myself into the international community' and 'I will be able to communicate anywhere in the world.' To become such a person would be very prestigious: 'A good English speaker from my country is a well-educated person' and 'A good English speaker is respected for his abilities and enjoys an advantage over the less fortunate ones.'

ITAs from this group must make choices of great subtlety and difficulty. To be aware of a gap between the English they have used for many years and the English they need to use to teach and to socialise does not require a choice. But being willing to explore and fill in that gap does. For many ITAs who rightly feel that they are already native English speakers, having to re-think and re-tool their English use is a kind of personal affront. If the university and state assessments say that their English is good enough to teach, why should they have to make further efforts at the expense of time that could be spent on study in their own disciplines? Nonetheless, some ITAs from this group choose to move beyond this intrapersonal conflict, and seek out ESL professionals on the campus and ask for advice and materials for self-study. It should be noted here that to change one's suprasegmental pronunciation of a second language presents a significant cognitive challenge, and requires persistence over time. Some report becoming more proactive in conversations they have with other English speakers by asking for clarification of unfamiliar words, but this is something that must be done with delicacy. Too many interruptions in conversations with the wrong people may mean friction with those higher in the university hierarchy or loss of face in front of students. In terms of pronunciation problems, think of how difficult it must be to ask a colleague or students to give consistent feedback on pronunciation, yet this is what a few ITAs report doing. Further, just how these feedback sequences would fit in with actual teaching routines is a significant question, particularly in courses where ITAs are required to teach a large amount of content quickly, and in terms of teacher authority roles.

Whatever choices ITAs from this group make, it frequently means less time for study and research in their fields. Even with their strong desire to fit in locally and learn to communicate at an international level, some ITAs fear that their choices may result in alienation from L1 friends: 'My friends might think I want to be superior to them' or 'My friends in India will find it artificial, and they might think that I am showing off.' ITAs from 'institutional L2' contexts often report that they plan to work as academics or businessmen and women in international settings. For success in these careers, a decision must be made to become conversant in international affairs and events. One Indian ITA who recently began an internship with Intel in New Mexico reported that he had to watch the national and local news nightly to gain insights on what his American colleagues were talking about. Such internationally minded ITAs may help further develop the economies of their home countries by acting as key interfacers between interests in their home countries and international corporations. Language planners and policy makers in ITAs' home countries may be influenced to emphasise more widely accessible educational programmes which teach English as an international language, with pronunciation placed in the curriculum.

Conclusion

Adult bilinguals who become teachers in their second languages make many choices in response to specific contexts. These choices have implications for them personally in terms of their language development, their goals, their emotional lives, their identities and their relationships with others. Their choices have implications for them professionally, and because they operate as teachers in their second languages, their choices are felt by their students, by the educational systems they work in and by wider society. Adult bilinguals' choices are further constrained by the language-learning context in which they learned the second language they are using to teach. These language-learning contexts (see Siegel 2003) can be seen as expressions of an educational culture in operation in a given country. Yet current theories on culture suggest that people are not 'programmed' with 'cultural rules' but are in fact individuals 'who are motivated by personal concerns and riven with difficulties in making decisions' (Gonzalez 2004, 21). Thus, regardless of how bilinguals who teach in a second language learned their second language, some, regardless of their country of origin and educational experience, formulate and use specific social strategies to succeed. These strategies are social in that these adult bilinguals seek out and exploit real-time, real-life, professionally focused opportunities to interact with native and other speakers of the second language. These opportunities are also used as venues for pushed output, in which adult bilinguals can work out cognitively what they wish to say for extended periods of time, while paying careful attention. A focus on this population of second language users has real potential for exploring the role of language socialisation in second language acquisition, particularly in researching intersections between context and social strategies consciously applied (see Watson-Gegeo and Nielsen 2003).

It is my hope that second and foreign languages in all language-learning contexts across the globe can be extended to all learners who wish to learn languages for social, economic, political and personal reasons. Children acquiring two or more languages are likely to constitute a majority on a global scale (Genesee 2001). It makes sense to consider where children learning second and foreign languages will end up as adults, and what choices they will have to make as they cross international borders and take up a variety of professions using a second language. The time to begin making second-language learners and their parents and communities aware of those choices is now.

Acknowledgements

I wish to thank Dale T. Griffee, Vu Lee Ho and Emmanuel Nenghabi for their timely assistance. I am also grateful to Premakumari Dheram for pushing me in the research direction I needed to go in.

References

Cohen, D.K. and J.P. Spillane. 1992. Policy and Practice: The Relations between Governance and Instruction. *Review of Research in Education* 18: 3–49.

Davis, W. 1991. International Teaching Assistants and Cultural Differences: Student Evaluations of Rapport, Approachability, Enthusiasm and Fairness. In *Preparing the Professoriate of Tomorrow to Teach*, eds. J. Nyquist, et al. Dubuque, IA: Kendall Hunt.

Freeman, D., and J.C. Richards. 1993. Conceptions of Teaching and the Education of Second Language Teachers. *TESOL Quarterly* 27(2): 193–216.

Genesee, F. 2001. Bilingual First Language Acquisition: Exploring the Limits of the Language Faculty. *Annual Review of Applied Linguistics* 21: 153–168.

Gonzales, N. 2004. Disciplining the Discipline: Anthropology and the Pursuit of Quality Education. *Educational Researcher* 33(5): 17–25.

Gorsuch, G.J. 1993. Brave Use of English Pays Off. *The Daily Yomiuri*, May 2, p. 9.

________ 1998. Yakudoku EFL Instruction in Two Japanese High School Classrooms: An Exploratory Study. *JALT Journal* 20(1): 6–30.

________ 2000. EFL Educational Policies and Educational Cultures: Influences on Teachers' Approval of Communicative Activities. *TESOL Quarterly* 34(4): 675–710.

________ 2003. The Educational Cultures of International Teaching Assistants and U.S. Universities. TESL-EJ 7(3): 1–17. http://writing.berkeley.edu/TESL-EJ/ej27/a1.html.

Holliday, A. 1994. *Appropriate Methodology and Social Context*. Cambridge: Cambridge University Press.

Law, G. 1995. Ideologies of English language Education in Japan. *JALT Journal*, 17: 213–224.

Lortie, D.C. 1975. *Schoolteacher: A Sociological Study*. Chicago: University of Chicago Press.

Ornstein, A. and F. Hunkins. 1993. *Curriculum: Foundations, Principles and Issues*. 2nd ed. Boston: Allyn and Bacon.

Siegel, J. 2003. Social Context. In *The Handbook of Second Language Acquisition*, eds. C. Doughty and M. Long. Malden, MA: Blackwell Publishing.

Snow, C. 1993. Bilingualism and Second Language Acquisition. In *Pyscholinguistics*, eds. J. Berko Gleason and N. Ratner. Fort Worth, TX: Harcourt Brace.

Valdez, G. 1998. The World Outside and Inside Schools: Language and Immigrant Children. *Educational Researcher* 27(6): 4–18.

Wada, M. and T. Cominos. 1994. Language Policy and the JET Program. In *Studies in Team Teaching*, eds. M. Wada & T. Cominos. Tokyo: Kenkyusha.

Wang, Y., M. Martin and S. Martin. 2002. Understanding Asian Graduate Students' English Literacy Problems. *College Teaching* 50(3): 97–101.

Watson-Gegeo, K.A. and S. Nielsen. 2003. Language Socialization in SLA. In *The Handbook of Second Language Acquisition*, eds. C. Doughty and M. Long Malden, MA: Blackwell Publishing.

Yukawa, E. 1994. Team Teaching and Changes in Teaching Routines in a Japanese High School Reading Classroom. In *Studies in Team Teaching*, eds. M. Wada and T. Cominos. Tokyo: Kenkyusha.

15

Higher Education and Gender in Pakistan: Issues and Concerns for Language Planning

Sabiha Mansoor

Pakistan with a population of 148.72 million (*Economic Survey* 2003–2004) is one of the largest Muslim countries in the world. The literacy rate in 2003 was estimated at 54 % with 66.25% males and 41.75% females (ibid.). The country lags behind the other South Asian countries in both elementary and secondary education. In higher education (which includes undergraduate and postgraduate studies) the participation rate is a mere 3% as compared to the 50% participation rate in the advanced countries.

In 2001–2002, females had less access to higher education, regarded today as a capital investment (*Economic Survey* 2003–2004). In the 939 science and arts colleges with an enrollment of 7,51,000 students, there were only 394 women's colleges with an enrollment of 3,70,000 female students. In the 374 professional colleges with an enrollment of 1,61,349 students throughout the country, the gap gets wider with only 20 women's professional colleges having an enrollment of 40,540. Many of the other professional colleges are co-education colleges. According to the latest Higher Education Commission (2004) release, there are 53 universities and 8 degree-awarding institutions in the public sector with a total enrollment of 3,88,668 (2,20,620 male and 1,68,048 female) students and 30 universities and 15 degree-awarding institutions in the private sector with an enrollment of 16,410 male and female students. The total enrollment in the universities is 0.62% in the age group 17–23 of the population (*Economic Survey,* 1999–2000).

Status of women in Pakistani society

Women do not seem to have access to higher education in Pakistan as their choices are constrained by several factors that include limited access to parental wealth and public funds for higher education that are typically far less than that for men. Further, personal returns from higher education to men in terms of income and social mobility are invariably higher than that to women (see Ali 1998; Sadker and Sadker 1994).

Pakistani women face similar problems in terms of socioeconomic status and employment also. According to a study conducted by the National Commission on the Status of Women (Rizvi 2003), it was lamentable that though women in Pakistan constituted about 50% of the total population, their participation in the public sector was marginal. Overall, the major contribution of women in the employment sector was in agriculture (66%), followed by industry (12%). The participation of women in the service sector was marginal (23%) and the report says that there is no existing government policy which facilitates women entering government jobs. Again, according to an analytical paper prepared by the multi-support unit of the Social Action Programme in Pakistan in 2000 (ibid.), a severe gender imbalance in favour of males exists at all top, senior and middle management levels across all government departments in each province/area.

Focus of study

The study focuses on some of the key areas in language planning and language education. Both approaches, namely, quantitative and qualitative were considered to examine which would be more suitable, and a 'combined approach' (Robson 1973) was adopted since the main purpose was not only to find out the numbers and percentages of respondents who held the same or different attitudes, values, opinions and beliefs, but also the reasons for the same. The subject of this study was language education in Pakistan, and the techniques used to study the differences in language attitudes and language use among students, parents and teachers were questionnaire surveys, interviews and documentary analysis. The study was designed to be a 'real world enquiry' mainly concerned with contributing to both language policy and practice in higher education in Pakistan. The concern in this article is with the former as it relates to women only.

Sample

A minimum sample of 2,450 students was required for this study with a level of significance (∝) of 5% and a power of 80%, using multistage cluster sampling with stratification. The sample of the colleges and universities from private and public (government) as well as general and professional was taken from the list of degree colleges and universities as listed in the Handbook of Colleges of Pakistan (University Grants Commission 1999). A decision was taken by the researcher to select the colleges and universities only from the capital cities of Pakistan and the federal capital Islamabad.

Results

Background characteristics

The sample obtained, of 2,136 students, was predominantly from Punjab (Lahore and Taxila), Sindh (Karachi and Hyderabad), Balochistan (Quetta), the federal capital (Islamabad), and the NWFP (Peshawar). Data was collected from 121 subject and English teachers from all provinces except Balochistan. Only 63 questionnaires of parents were received from Punjab and Sindh. The profile of the students according to the type of their institutions shows that the majority of them (84%), were from colleges and a smaller number (16%) from universities. Also, around two-thirds (66 %) of all students in the study were from public sector institutions. The majority of the students (42%), reported Urdu as their mother tongue, followed by Punjabi (30%), Pushto (14%), Balochi (5%), Sindhi (4%) and others (5%). The results of the study show that the students involved in higher education in Pakistan belong to various socioeconomic backgrounds (income groups, divided into quintiles). Students studying in private sector institutions have significantly higher monthly household incomes as compared to students studying in those run by the public sector.

Language competency

In terms of gender, a significant difference in males and females is found in the competency of speaking regional languages. The results show that males are more competent than females in speaking regional languages, while no significant difference is seen in the competency of the two sexes in writing regional languages.

Urdu is considered as a national language in Pakistan. More than half of all students apart from those speaking Sindhi claim a high level of spoken and written proficiency in Urdu. In terms of gender, a significant difference is found in males and females in the competency of speaking Urdu. The results show that females claim higher degrees of competency than males in speaking Urdu. A marginally significant difference in males and females is also seen with regard to the competency in writing Urdu. Results show that females claim to be more competent than males in writing Urdu as well. Most of the teachers and parents claim higher proficiency in spoken than in written Urdu.

English is considered an international as well as official language in Pakistan. Results show that despite this, the majority of students do not claim to have high spoken or written proficiency in English and report their proficiency in spoken English to be lower than their written proficiency. No significant difference is found between males and females with regard to competency in speaking English. A significant difference between males and females is seen in their competence in written English. The results show that males claim higher proficiency than females in writing English, but their overall competence in English is low in relation to its importance as an international language and the fact that all students have studied English as a compulsory subject from seven (in public sector schools) to twelve years (in private sector schools).

Language use

Significant associations were found between language use and gender. The study revealed that in the family, there were differences in language use in different domains according to gender, with males reporting maximum use of mother tongue and regional languages, and females reporting maximum use of Urdu and English. Among friends, males again reported using mostly the mother tongue and regional language, while females reported more use of Urdu. With teachers, males reported using mainly the mother tongue, the regional language and English, while in the case of females, it was Urdu. A similar trend was found in their interactions with fellow students, office/bank employees and while visiting another province.

As seen in the results, fathers reported higher use of mother tongue in all domains as compared to mothers. More use of the regional language was also reported among fathers while talking to office/bank employees or visiting other provinces. The mothers reported using more of Urdu while talking to friends. They also reported more use of English with the family or with children. A major reason for this gender-based difference in attitudes, as shown by various studies, including the present one, is the attitudes towards different languages among female students, parents and teachers, who display more positive attitudes to 'high-status' languages, such as Urdu and English and less positive attitudes to 'low-status' languages, such as the regional languages in Pakistan.

Language attitudes

An overwhelming majority of students, male and female, from all provinces (in both public and private sectors), teachers and parents show highly positive attitudes to English as indicated by their preference for English as a medium of instruction in higher education. Female students gave more weight to different instrumental as well as integrative reasons as compared to male students except for travelling abroad, getting access to international books and journals, living and behaving like English-speaking Pakistanis, becoming friendly with English-speaking Pakistanis, and getting acquainted with people in touch with the latest trends in the West. Prominent among the instrumental reasons given was that fluency in English helped students cope better with college/university classes and in future careers. The integrative reasons students considered significant included acquiring new ideas and broadening their outlook as well as improving their social status, with female students giving more weight to these reasons than male students.

Gender and sociocultural (language shift) factors

An important factor in language spread or language shift is the relative economic, political and cultural co-variation principle. Punjabi children from lower social backgrounds perceive that everyone who uses Punjabi occupies a relatively low position, and everyone using Urdu or English occupies a higher one. Hence, language is seen as the cause of differential status. This perception may be strengthened by in-group members who have moved up socially and are now occupying positions of higher status. It appears therefore that the upper classes and the elite are moving away from Punjabi. Urdu and English are seen as languages of a future urbanised society. English is particularly seen as modern and progressive, and attracts Punjabi speakers, including rural Punjabis, who have moved into urban areas to shift linguistically into these language groups, thereby speeding up the process of language shift. The results of this study also make explicit the attitudes of parents and teachers. Both parents and teachers display highly positive attitudes towards English. Working-class parents see school as an avenue for their upward mobility of their children. The choice of schooling —depending on whether parents prefer to send their children to English-medium or Urdu-medium schools—encourages children to speak the respective languages. The phenomenon of parents helping their children learn the 'correct' language (in this study, Urdu and English, and not Punjabi) so as not to be stigmatised later in life and to advance socially and materially is widespread. This is the main reason for Punjabi parents not transmitting their language to the next generation. It is seen that the languages commonly used for teacher–student communication in colleges are English and Urdu. It seems that Punjabi is rarely used for interaction between college teachers and students although it is their mother tongue. The results also showed more use of Punjabi by parents, many of whom have not transmitted their mother tongue to their children.

The results also show a trend among Sindhi-speaking students to move away from their mother tongue, with Urdu being used more than Sindhi, not only in the formal domain but also in the informal domain among family and friends. These results are indicative of the lack of attention being paid to Sindhi in terms of improving its status in the official sphere as well as in developing materials for educational purposes, and the situation could gradually lead to a language shift, as happened in the case of Punjabi students, if steps are not taken by the state to address this issue.

State policies: assimilation versus integration

The language shift among many urban-educated regional speakers may be seen as a result of the 'assimilation' policy being followed by the state—where Urdu as the 'dominant language' is replacing other 'minority languages'—rather than an 'integration policy' which aims at 'cultural pluralism,' where all languages co-exist side by side, without feeling 'endangered' or becoming extinct (see Skutnabb-Kangas 2000). Pakistan, since its independence in 1947, has been following a policy of giving a tremendous boost to Urdu as the national language. Urdu enjoys a high status and is used along with English for all official purposes. Additionally, Urdu followed by English, is used most in social institutions (primarily schools) and in the mass media, especially newspapers and television, which help in the spread of the language. English also enjoys a great deal of institutional support in Pakistan and is also the language of trade and commerce. One of the important factors responsible for the rapid assimilation of Punjabi in urban areas is the lack of institutional support.

Gender issues

A large majority of female students in higher education in Pakistan report limited competency in the use of their mother tongues and regional languages. They also display little or no interest in their mother tongues and regional languages due to the low status given to these languages and the limited role they have in the country's official domain, thereby accelerating the process of language shift amongst regional speakers.

The results underscore the importance of social structure, identity and ethnolinguistic vitality of the speakers as some of the primary factors responsible for the tendencies discussed above amongst the ethnic-minority female students, particularly Punjabi students, in this research study. The plight of women is a matter of great concern in South Asian countries, such as India and Bangladesh, where studies have been conducted on minority rights, identity and gender in relation to language variation and language use. Some of the South Asian studies such as Sankaranarayanan (2001) and Guhathakurta (2003) have also underscored the importance of these factors in terms of gender and language use.

The low self-esteem of Pakistani female students may be attributed to their low social and economic status in society. This in turn is related to their unequal participation in higher education and employment, particularly in the upper ranks of public and private sector institutions and organisations, as compared to their male counterparts. These problems are further compounded by the social and religious taboos that confine women in Islamic countries, such as Pakistan, and prevent them from becoming liberated and empowered. This sense of deprivation is further enhanced by the low ethnolinguisitic vitality of regional speakers, especially those speaking Punjabi (see Mansoor 1993; 2005). The Pakistani female students therefore see their English medium education and fluency in English and Urdu, that are high status languages, as being advantageous to them. In other words, learning English appears to be the key to empowerment in terms of improving socioeconomic status and becoming modern and broadminded by gaining access to the latest ideas in the West.

Recommendations

The female population of a country has a vital role to play in transmitting the mother tongue to the next generation, and in ensuring its preservation and vitality. It is thus highly recommended that measures be taken by the state to protect women's rights to higher education and employment, which would not only lead to an improvement in their economic and social status as well as their self-esteem but would also help in promoting positive attitudes towards their mother tongues and regional languages, thereby arresting the process of language shift amongst the ethnic-minority female speakers.

References

Ali, M. A. 1998. Women and Higher Education in the 21st Century. In *Higher education: A Pathway to Development,* eds. J. Talati et al. Karachi: Oxford University Press.

Government of Pakistan. 2000. *Economic Survey 2003–2004*. Islamabad: Finance Division, Government of Pakistan.

________. 2000(a) *Economic Survey 1999–2000*. Islamabad: Finance Division, Government of Pakistan.

Guhathakurta, M. 2003. Minority Rights, Identity Politics and Gender in Bangladesh: Current Problems and Issues. In *Adhunika,* ed. R. Khundkar. http://www.adhunika.org/issues/minority Rights MT.html.

Mansoor, S. 1993. *Punjabi, Urdu, English in Pakistan: A Sociolinguistic Study*. Lahore: Vanguard.

________. 2005. *Language Planning in Higher Education: A Case Study of Pakistan*. Karachi: Oxford University Press.

Rizvi, M. 2003. *Inquiry Report on Status of Women Employment in Public Sector Organizations*. National Commission on the Status of Women, Government of Pakistan.

Sadker, M., and D. Sadker. 1994. *Failing at Fairness: How Our Schools Cheat Girls*. New York: Simon & Schuster.

Sankaranarayanan, G. 2001. Gender Bias in an Indian Language Variation. In *Language in India*, ed. M.S. Thirumalai. http://www.languageinindia.com/sep2001/genderndlang.html.

Skutnabb-Kangas, T. 2000. *Linguistic Genocide in Education – or Worldwide Diversity and Human Rights?* Mahwah, N J: Lawrence Erlbaum.

University Grants Commission. 1999. *Handbook of Colleges of Pakistan*. Islamabad: University Grants Commission of Pakistan.

16

Merging of Context and Methodology: MEd in the TESOL Curriculum in Sri Lanka: A Pioneering Effort

Marie Perera

Introduction

This paper examines a curriculum that endeavours to bridge the gap between 'metropolitan' and 'peripheral' contexts and merge methodology and context. First, I will provide a brief background to the recent debate on the need to move towards more 'context-sensitive' language pedagogy. Next, I will discuss the Sri Lankan English Language Teaching (ELT) scenario against this background and present briefly the proposed master of education programme in Teaching of English to Speakers of Other Languages (MEd in TESOL) at the Faculty of Education, University of Colombo, which attempts to contextualise ELT within a Sri Lankan as well as an Asian context.

Context and methodology in ELT

There is an ongoing debate on whether the dominance of communicative language teaching (CLT) has led to the neglect of one of the crucial aspects of language pedagogy, namely, the context in which that pedagogy takes place (Bax 2003). While some argue that there is a need to replace a methodological approach to language pedagogy with a context approach (see ibid.), others think that these two aspects could work in harmony (see Harmer 2003).

Holliday (1994), who made a distinction between two main ELT sectors—that is, British, Australian and North American (BANA) and tertiary, secondary and primary (TESP)—suggests that most of the intellectual 'technology' of ELT has originated in the BANA countries. He argues that in curriculum development based on such 'technology', insufficient attention has been paid to the needs of the TESP students. On the other hand, when course developers deviate from the BANA 'ideal' such attempts are labelled as deficit. Thus, Holliday's argument is that each language-teaching context needs 'to be analysed constructively in *local* terms and not on the basis of *a priori* judgements of value or efficacy developed in other contexts' (Tudor 1996, 131).

One of the reasons for the failure of the teacher education programmes for non-BANA professionals is that these courses are built primarily on theories and methodologies developed on the basis of research conducted in western countries (Kachru 1994; Liu 1998; Sridhar 1994). Comparatively, not much attempt has been made to collect data from other contexts (Kachru 1994) and as a result, the 'vast millions of L2 users who learn and use the second language in their own countries' are left out from this database (Sridhar 1994, 801).

Thus, if teacher education programmes are to be of service to the non-BANA professionals, the theoretical foundation of such courses needs to be adapted. In other words, the trainees should be able to adapt the knowledge they gain to suit their own contexts.

Even though there is general agreement that the non-BANA countries should develop their own ESL curriculum to suit their own contexts, they seem to have a conscious or unconscious 'deficit' attitude. Hence, most of these countries seek the help of 'experts' from the West to develop their curriculum and learning material. There develops an 'us–them' perception where the 'us', the experts, tend to believe that the 'them' 'don't know the technology' (Holliday 2001, 174) and are easily dominated. The work of Swales (1980) on the influence of sociopolitical environment on ESL and that of Coleman (1996) on the influence of society on what happens in the classroom emphasises the fact that non-BANA countries should look to their own local experts to develop their curricula and teaching material.

In most Asian cultures, which have a long tradition of considering the teacher as 'authority', the role of the teacher is considered not as a facilitator but as a 'fount of knowledge'. Thus, English teaching in Asia is still dominantly didactic, product oriented and teacher centred (Campbell and Zhao 1993). Consequently, BANA's teaching methods, materials and programmes often face a 'tissue rejection' (Holliday 1992) in Asia, as shown by Burnaby and Sun (1989), Canagarajah (1993), Liu (1998) and Pennycook (1989).

The available literature suggests that the teaching of English in Sri Lanka is not satisfactory and does not meet the needs of the majority of Sri Lankan students. In this context, a brief overview of the historical development of ELT in Sri Lanka may be useful.

Historical development of English as a second language prior to Independence

Sri Lanka's (then, Ceylon's) introduction to the English language was linked with colonisation. As a British colony, English became the dominant language used for administrative purposes in the courts and in all areas of business and trade. Thus, a need arose to establish English medium schools. The missionaries had already established schools where the instruction was provided in the mother tongue. With the establishment of English medium schools, two types of schools evolved—the 'English schools', where the medium of instruction was English, and the 'vernacular' schools, where the medium of instruction was the indigenous languages, Sinhala and Tamil. The English schools, in spite of being subsidised by the state, were fee levying and as a result were available only to the affluent classes. On the other hand, the vernacular schools were meant for the children of the masses, and the education provided was free, but of very low quality (Jayasuriya 1967).

To teach English, the English schools adopted the materials and methods that were in use in England at that time. All teachers, those who taught English as a subject as well as others, were competent in English and the number of teachers required was few.

The first step in making English available to the masses was taken in 1943, when a special committee appointed by the state council proposed for the first time that English be introduced as a second language in all primary schools where it was not the language of instruction. In primary schools where English was the language of instruction, Sinhalese or Tamil was to be the second language subject.

Teaching of English after Independence

With the decision to teach English in all schools from grade four, a heavy responsibility fell on the State to provide the necessary facilities. Although the government embarked on this new policy, it seems to have done so without the full realisation of the problems involved. No concrete proposals were made regarding how to teach English as a second language (De Lanerolle Commission Report 1973, 34).

With the new policy, English had to be made available in all schools. However, the number of competent teachers available was not sufficient to cater to this demand. Consequently, English classes were started when teachers with minimum qualifications were available. This created a new problem—the supply of teachers (ibid.). One of the chief causes identified for the deterioration of standards of English was that it was not taught by trained teachers (De Silva Committee Report 1960). A specialist training college wasopened, modelled on those established in the West to train teachers of English. However, this was not sufficient to cater to the demand as indicated by the evidence of various reports (De Lanerolle Commission Report 1973; the First Report of the National Education Commission 1992; the White Paper 1981) which continued to mention that teacher training was inadequate.

Due to the nationalisation of schools, English medium schools were now available to the masses. As a result, students who had not studied English earlier, and those who were not exposed to English at home were in the same classes as those who knew English. Therefore, the English medium schools had to face the problem of heterogeneity in the student population.

When it was found that the expected result of English being available to all was not being achieved, various committees were appointed by the successive governments to look into the defects of the education system and especially into the teaching of English, and as a result, various curricular reforms were proposed. The next section of this paper will examine some of the major proposals and curricular changes pertaining to the teaching of English during the period after English was made a second language.

Curricular reforms and the teaching of English as a second language

The first measures to address the issue of how to teach English as a second language were undertaken in 1953. A syllabus was prepared for the teaching of English to primary school students, which was based on 'literature on the teaching of English to immigrants in Australia' (De Lanerolle Commission Report 1973, 55). This syllabus does not appear to have helped teachers very much as school inspectors reported that in the majority of the schools, teaching English as a second language was not successful (ibid). There was no prescribed methodology and different textbooks were used in different schools. Although there was a syllabus, the teachers did not know how to teach it. Therefore, they followed the same methodology as was used to teach English as a first language.

A committee set up in 1957 suggested that a group of experts be appointed to prepare syllabuses (De Silva Committee Report 1960). The committee also noted that there was no satisfactory series of English textbooks available for the primary and post-primary classes. It was recommended that 'textbooks should be produced to suit our country' (ibid., 18). Further, it suggested some guidelines based on the 'direct method', which was claimed to have been successfully used to teach modern languages in other parts of the world. However, it was not a success in Sri Lanka: 'The 1963 scheme was unrealistic and difficult to implement and confusion continued' (De Lanerolle Commission Report 1973, 68).

In 1965, a new set of textbooks, *An English Course,* prepared by the ministry of education became the standard prescription at all schools in the country. It was assumed that English would be used mainly as a means for additional reading at universities (Cumaranatunga 1989; Mosback 1984), and the stated objective of the ESL programme in schools at that time was to develop reading comprehension. On the other hand, the textbooks were written based on the graded structural approach (Cumaranatunga 1989). Hence, once again there was a mismatch between the stated objectives of the ESL programme and the instructional materials developed to achieve them. The majority of teachers claimed that the content was 'uninteresting', the methodology 'artificial', and the learning, 'mechanical' (De Lanerolle Commission Report 1973, 65).

Even though the textbooks were locally produced, the approach and methodology used appeared to be foreign, and there seemed to be little improvement in the standard of English. This idea is supported by Jayasuriya (1969, 69), who stated that 'compulsory English for all children in and above standard three is one of the greatest deceptions perpetrated on the people of this country'.

In the early 1980s, against the backdrop of the communicative language teaching (CLT) fever in the West, the general view was that the language-teaching methodology used in Sri Lanka at that time was not catering to the learner's need to be able to communicate in the second language. There was growing concern that both the existing English textbooks and the methodology used were not equipping young people with the ability to communicate in English (Cumaranatunga 1989; De Silva 1979). In late October 1982, it was decided to produce a new set of textbooks, *English Every Day* (*EED*), based on CLT. According to Mosback (1990, 19), who was the British consultant for the textbook-writing project, 'all the teachers and students in the country were introduced to the principles on which the course would be based' through workshops.

However, classroom research based on the *EED* series shows that CLT has not produced expected results (Perera 2002; Silva 1993). Silva (1993), for example, discusses the impact of the cultural implications of teacher/pupil perceptions of the role of classroom interaction which hinders the implementation of CLT.

With the introduction of the *EED* materials, an attempt was made to change the traditional teaching practices and provide the teachers with guidelines regarding their classroom practices. However, it also made some teachers anxious as they were unable to follow some of the guidelines, in the contexts in which they taught. Therefore, rather than prescribing general guidelines, it seemed important that teacher education should address the complexities of teaching English in different contexts and encourage teacher flexibility and initiative.

With the dawn of the twenty-first century in concurrence with the general educational reforms taking place in Sri Lanka, another set of textbooks and curriculum have been introduced once again under the guidance of 'foreign experts'. It may be still premature to analyse this curriculum. The teacher's guide states that 'no one single' English language teaching–learning approach or ideology is recommended. 'However, the Experiential (also identified as 'Constructivist') Approach to teaching–learning, which has in recent times enjoyed a renaissance, is definitely favoured' (Poole 2003, 6). According to Poole, even though the current national curriculum for English language learning in Sri Lankan public schools advocates experiential/constructivist (E/C) attitudes and practices, what is actually being used in the classrooms and promoted in continuing education is predominately the behavioral approach. He stresses that it is vital for educators to be able to identify why the E/C approach is so difficult to implement in Sri Lankan schools in the existing teaching–learning conditions and teacher–student dynamics, even though teaching–learning practices established in the new 'modernised' curriculum are modelled on it.

As can be seen from the above discussion, one of the reasons identified repeatedly for this unsatisfactory state of ELT in Sri Lanka is the lack of competent ESL teachers. Attempts have been made to find ways of improving the teaching of English by changing the curriculum regularly, based on western models. The reasons for the low rate of success in the teaching of English could be in part due to the methodology used to train teachers, who are not equipped with the tools needed to understand the context in which learning and teaching take place and to adopt the methods to suit the context.

One of the grave problems in the Sri Lankan ELT field is the lack of teacher educators. Although there are several institutions that train teachers, only the National Institute of Education conducts training programmes for teacher educators, and these too are short-term programmes. The gravity of the problem is illustrated from the statistics provided by the ministry of education regarding the teacher centres. As part of the proposed reforms in general education, one hundred teachers centres have been established throughout the country. However, there are only nine ELT teacher educators appointed to impart training in these centres! It was in this context that the Faculty of Education, University of Colombo, proposed the Master of Education (TESOL) curriculum.

Master of Education, TESOL

At present, none of the universities in Sri Lanka offers a masters degree in TESOL. The faculty of education in the University of Colombo offers a one-year postgraduate diploma course in education (Teaching of English as a Second Language) to graduate ESL teachers. This qualification provides them with the basic professional qualifications needed to function as ESL teachers in the education system. However, without at least a masters degree, teachers are unable to proceed further in their professional development. On the other hand, the system badly needs ESL teacher educators, and that need is also not catered to, due to the non-availability of a masters degree programme in TESOL. Therefore, the present programme is developed in response to the need of its target student population, and as the curriculum indicates, it uses a context-specific approach.

Conclusion

The MEd in the TESOL curriculum is a small step in the right direction in trying to find remedies for the ills of ESL teaching in Sri Lanka. However, progress in this pioneering effort will depend on how successful we are in facing the challenges. Most SAARC countries would have faced similar challenges in the past, if not at present, and collaborating with them is expected to have a positive influence on the approach to ESL across the region.

References

Bax, S. 2003. Bringing Context and Methodology Together. *ELT Journal* Vol. 57/3: 295–296.

Burnaby, B and Y. Sun. 1989. Chinese Teachers' Views of Western Language Teaching: Context Informs Paradigms. *TESOL Quarterly* 23/2: 219–38.

Campbell, K. and Y. Zhao. 1993. The Dilemma of English Language Instruction in the People's Republic of China. *TESOL Journal* 4/2: 4–6.

Canagarajah, S. 1993. Critical Ethnography of a Sri Lankan Classroom: Ambiguities in Student Opposition to Reproduction through ESOL. *TESOL Quarterly* 27/4: 601–21.

Coleman, H. 1996. *Society and the Language Classroom*. Cambridge: Cambridge University Press.

Cumaranatunga, L. 1989. *Designing Instructional Materials to Meet Local Needs.* Paper presented at the International Conference on English in South Asia, Islamabad, Pakistan. January 4–9.

De Lanerolle Commission. 1973. *Report of the Committee of Inquiry into the Teaching of English in the Schools of Sri Lanka.* Colombo: Government Printing Press.

De Silva, A. 1979. Content and Methodology. In *Socio- economic and Other Factors Affecting the Teaching of English*, Colombo: Sri Lanka Foundation Institute.

De Silva, S. F. 1960. *Report of the Committee of Inquiry into the Teaching of English in Ceylon Schools. Sessional Paper V.* Colombo: Government Publication Bureau.

National Education Commission. 1992. *The First Report of the National Education Commission. Sessional Paper V.* Colombo: Government Printing Press.

Harmer, J. 2003. Popular Culture, Methods, and Context. *ELT Journal* Vol. 57/3: 289–294.

Holliday, A. 1994. *Appropriate Methodology and Social Context.* Cambridge: Cambridge University Press.

Holliday, A. 2001. Achieving Cultural Continuity in Curriculum Innovation. In *Innovation in English Language Teaching: A Reader*, eds. D.R. Hall and A. Hewings. London: Routledge in association with Macquarie University and The Open University.

Jayasuriya, J. E. 1969. *Education in Ceylon since Independence.* Colombo: Lakehouse.

Kachru, Y. 1994. Monolingual Bias in SL Research. *TESOL Quarterly* 23/4: 795–800.

Liu, D. 1998. Ethnocentrism in TESOL: Teacher Education and the Neglected Needs of International TESOL Students. *ELT Journal Volume* 52/1: 3–10.

Mosback, G. 1984. Making a Structure-based Course More Communicative. *ELT Journal* 38(3): 178–191.

Mosback, G. 1990. National Syllabus and Textbook Design on Communicative Principles - 'English Every Day'. *ELT Journal* 44(1): 18–24.

Pennycook, A. 1989. The Concept of Method Interested Knowledge, and Politics of Language Teaching. *TESOL Quarterly* 23/4: 589–618.

Perera, M. 2002. *Role of Classroom Interaction in Second Language Acquisition in Sri Lanka*. Unpublished Ph.D. Diss. University of Wollongong, Australia.

Poole, R. 2003. *Final Report of the Secondary Modernization Project – English Subject Component.* Maharagama: N.I.E.

Silva, J. 1993. *Classroom Interaction Patterns in a Few Varied ESL Teaching Contexts in Sri Lanka - A Comparative Study.* Unpublished Ph.D. Diss. University of Colombo, Sri Lanka.

Sridhar, S. 1994. A Reality Check for SLA Theories. *TESOL Quarterly* 28/4: 800–5.

Swales, J. 1980. The Educational Environment and its Relevance to ESP Programme Design. In *Projects in Material Design, ELT Documents Special*. London: The British Council.

Tudor, I. 1996. *Learner-Centeredness as Language Education*. Cambridge: Cambridge University Press.

The White Paper. 1981. *Educational Proposals for Reform - General, University and Tertiary*. Colombo: Ministry of Education.

17

Towards a Culturally-Friendly Approach to ESL Teacher Development in Bangladesh

Arifa Rahman

Introduction

In recent years, a general sense of the recognition of the teacher as being at the heart of the educational process has emerged. The greater the importance attached to education as a whole—whether for cultural transmission, for social cohesion and justice, or for the human resource development so critical in modern, technology-based economies—the higher is the priority that needs to be accorded to the teachers responsible for that education. Teachers are being seen as the ultimate key to educational change and learning improvement. It is therefore reasonable to argue that the need for an effective provision to initiate, develop and sustain teachers through an appropriate process of education should be amongst the highest priorities of educational planning.

Models of language teacher education range from a top-down transmissive scheme of craft knowledge through strong and weak forms of applied science models to a bottom-up reflective approach to teacher education. Although it is recognised that the latter models are favoured, it may also be argued that they might be inappropriate in an educational culture which might prefer to work in a more conservative and conformist way. A realistic approach to local settings would demand a reformulation of any given model to suit conditions of relevance. This view is crucial for arriving at appropriate teacher-education models for developing countries, and curriculum planners need to recognise this issue and incorporate this concept into the discourse of teacher training.

In the first part of this paper, I attempt a review of ELT policies and schemes and the changes undertaken in ESL teacher development over the last thirty years in Bangladesh. The second part develops an argument to formulate a framework for a culturally-friendly approach to English language teacher development.

ESL policies and ELT teacher development schemes

English in Bangladesh

Secession from Pakistan in 1971 ushered in a wave of nationalism which not only abolished Urdu, the national language in erstwhile East Pakistan, but also displaced English. Bengali, the predominant language, took precedence at all levels of the bureaucracy, education, administration and the judiciary. The Constitution, written in Bengali, declared that the state language would be Bengali (Part 1, Article 3). Later, in 1987, the *Bangla Procholon Ain* (Bengali Implementation Act) was passed to enforce the use of the language in all spheres. There was, however, no mention regarding the status of English.

In the education sector, in order to assert Bengali identity, English was abolished from the primary stage and withdrawn from the tertiary level in 1972. However, it remained a compulsory subject in secondary schools. Bengali was also made the medium of instruction in all schools. At the universities, all lectures were delivered in Bengali, though there was no accompanying effort for developing vernacular books or translations. This created immense difficulties particularly in the faculties of the sciences, medicine and engineering. In this way, policy dictates and nationalist fervour relegated English very rapidly to the background.

This language policy, clearly favouring Bengali, did not offer any directives with regard to English which had held powerful sway in the previous decades. Most importantly, there was no articulated policy for steps needed for the transition phase from English to Bengali. Perhaps because this transition phase was neither recognised nor discussed, English continued to survive like a smouldering fire. It is pertinent to point out that although all English medium schools were ordered to switch to Bengali, some private schools quietly continued to teach English and had long waiting lists for school places. Thus during the first decade, like its neighbours Pakistan, Sri Lanka and Nepal, Bangladesh felt the political need to discourage English amongst the masses and promote the national language. At the same time, it covertly provided opportunities for a small elite to develop and continue to be fluent in the language. English during this period survived in two forms—as a sterile but compulsory presence in the school curriculum and as a covert but robust form through the surreptitious patronage of an elitist minority (Rahman 1988). As Kachru (1996, 20) aptly describes, English in Bangladesh, like in other countries of this region, seemed at this period 'to be experiencing life after near-death'.

A decade on, a general sense of dissatisfaction over poor English standards in schools and in professions began to be voiced. Like its neighbours, Bangladesh began to wake up to the reality of an increasing importance of English in business, trade and technology, particularly in the ever-expanding private sector. Thus, previous nationalist arguments and anxieties about a colonial liability became muted in the face of English wielding the power of a modern-day asset. Even politicians who had actively campaigned for the use of the mother tongue (but privately sent their own children to English medium schools at home or preferably abroad), came forth with public comments about the need for English in the country. This is reminiscent of Michael West's argument of the instrumental function of the English language in Bengal in 1926 and, a century preceding that, Raja Ram Mohan Roy's plea for English education in India in 1823.

The status of ELT

The entire history of English Language Teaching (ELT) in Bangladesh has been a series of reformulations from time to time evident in the Education Commission and National Committee reports, memos and directives. The aim of reform and development undoubtedly has been the improvement of the quality and relevance of ELT. How far this has been the education ministry's clear objective and how far it has affected outcomes, however, need to be seriously evaluated.

In the decades following Independence, the focus has been on *quantity*—the temporal expansion of English learning. From year 6, English was extended down to year 3, and finally to year 1 in primary school. Having exhausted one end of the school continuum, the authorities introduced English into the first year of tertiary education with the result that general students now have thirteen years of English. These expansionist decisions have occasionally been tactics of crisis management. This emphasis on an uncontrolled educational expansion without a corresponding provision for trained teachers, teaching and learning facilities and other supporting infrastructure, has created an environment which is vulnerable to all sorts of problems, for example, the enormous pressure on almost non-existent resources in introducing English at the tertiary level. Nwagwu (1997, 87) claims that any society which stimulates uncoordinated growth of its education system and then fails to support this growth adequately creates 'an environment of crises'. Bangladesh is still a long way from matching action and resources to promises. Thus intentions, however well-meaning, often suffer from lack of planning and foresight, and the whims and exigencies of politicians and the bureaucracy.

ELT curricular reform

ELT curricular reform has been until recently a case of treating symptoms but ignoring the disease, which meant working without a clear and coordinated analysis of the entire situation and without incorporating factors such as the language competencies required of learners, the backwash effect of public examinations, the constraints on resources, and the adequate management of change, among other things. Changes in government, with each administration trying to take credit for fresh policies and ideas, have also had negative effects on long-term planning. For example, a feasibility study in the early nineties (Khan and Taylor 1993) recommended the establishment of regional English language centres. But this initiative was shelved for several years. Recently, it was channelled into the setting up of regional language laboratories, without any recognition of the fact that language laboratories are no longer considered useful and have been replaced by the idea of language learning centres which offer much more than just technical equipment.

With regard to the early efforts at curriculum renewal, the seventies and early eighties saw isolated efforts towards ELT reform, mostly by donor agencies. The focus was on the setting up of language laboratories at tertiary institutes and education extension centres. The laboratories were hardly used for any effective purpose and, with no maintenance or funding, merely went to waste. A 4-year English for Specific Purposes (ESP) curriculum unit was set up at the University of Dhaka. Needless to say, this too was not successful. As most reforms appeared to be linked to grants often tied to donor agendas that addressed covert market forces, they did not always coincide with national or local interests. At the same time, the local machinery worked with its own hidden agenda that thwarted reform attempts. Of course, this was not a unique feature to this region or to this particular field, as the literature on the management of educational innovation has recorded countless unsuccessful attempts (Markee 1997).

Since the mid-eighties there has been a realisation about long-term commitments with regard to coordinated reform, encouraged by interests in projectisation. The World Bank, the Asian Development Bank and the UNICEF have supported massive programmes for the revision of the syllabus and the textbooks at the primary level. At the secondary level, the British Overseas Development Agency (ODA, now called DFID) supported the revision of English textbooks for secondary schools together with the orientation of English language secondary-school teachers to the teaching of English as a foreign language (the OTEFL project).

ELT teacher development projects

During the eighties, the idea of the teacher as an essential element in the instructional process started to gain prominence, and hence efforts were made to develop teachers. Since the late eighties, there have been attempts to integrate educational insights into long- and short-term teacher development programmes. The major teacher development initiatives undertaken in Bangladesh are given below.

- *BEd Elective English Course:* The late eighties saw the syllabus revision of the BEd English specialisation course at the teacher training colleges (TTCs). Manuals for the trainer and the trainee were formulated. However, there was no follow-up of teaching procedures in the TTCs, and these rather well-written interactive lessons were exploited in the traditional lecture method. There is a widespread concern about the low enrolment figures in the English course of the BEd. The fact that other subjects are generally perceived as soft options impacts negatively on English.

- *(Secondary Science Educanion Development)* SSED: In the early nineties, this project included English teachers in its country-wide science teacher training scheme. However, the course content and methodology remained grammar based and traditional and dealt more with language items than with updating classroom pedagogy.
- *(English Language Teaching Improvement Project)* ELTIP: The now concluded 5-year ELTIP project adopted a participatory approach, in recognition of the difficulties of managing and sustaining change in education, particularly in developing societies with multifarious hidden agendas. Its goal was to improve the teaching of communicative English, which included teacher development, teaching materials improvement and testing reforms. A significant feature was an in-built research element. Khan (2003) evaluated the teacher training programme of ELTIP as being a step in the right direction, although dogged with constraints. At the end of the project in 2002, ELTIP resource centres established in TTCs remain a limping legacy of the once vibrant programme. Generally ignored by the TTC administration, they now operate in a limited way offering surface-scratching workshops arranged by the government for secondary school teachers from time to time. It is unfortunate that these centres are not being utilised to complement English teacher development in the TTCs. An EU-sponsored educational review report (PROMOTE 2004) has recommended active collaboration of the TTCs with the ELTIP resource centres and the PROMOTE resource centres.
- *(Programme to Motivate, Train and Employ Female Teachers in Rural Secondary Schools)* PROMOTE: A significant development in recent times, of a different nature, is the 7-year programme which has resource centres based at the eleven state-run TTCs. Again, it is PROMOTE's resource centres within the TTCs and their

link with the TTCs that is crucial to teacher development. PROMOTE has identified three shortage subject areas (mathematics, science and English language), for there are not enough trained teachers in secondary schools to teach these subjects. As a result, other subject area teachers often teach these courses.

- *(Secondary Education Sector Improvement Project)* SESIP: SESIP is currently collaborating with PROMOTE and the National University in the second revision of the English teaching studies component of the 2-year BEd course in the TTCs.
- *(National Curriculum and Textbook Board)* NCTB: As part of government involvement, the NCTB almost always acts as a partner in school projects. The NCTB has its own dominance over the system, and the politicisation of this organisation often wields a strong influence over policy and implementation. Nevertheless, it is fair to state that the NCTB runs its own orientation courses for teachers when new curricula and textbooks are introduced in schools, but as impact assessments are not carried out, their effectiveness cannot be judged. The NCTB has a track record of treating projects as one-off endeavours and launching new projects without linking them to previous efforts. As there is no serious evaluation or impact assessment studies, attempts are usually not made to build on former strengths to move forward.
- *Academic programmes:* In the field of English language teacher education, academic programmes are on offer at tertiary institutions in the public and private sectors. Although these are becoming increasingly popular, appropriate curriculum and quality assurance may be in doubt. Besides the regular BEd courses in the TTCs, some of the programmes in this area are
  - BELT (Bachelor in English Language Teaching): The Open University offers this 2-year distance education course. However, adverse conditions have affected negatively the proper and timely administration of this much-needed programme.
  - Dip-in-Ed (Diploma in Education): This 1-year postgraduate diploma course with an English component needs to incorporate a more contemporary approach to language teacher education.

- MEd: Unfortunately, a separate English option is not included at this level.
- MA in Applied Linguistics and ELT: Newly introduced, the course has yet to prove its worth.
- MA in ELT/TESOL/TEFL/TESL: Quality assurance is a crucial factor here and although programmes are approved by the University Grants Commission, a regulatory body needs to monitor the administration of these courses.

Planning a culturally appropriate ESL teacher development programme

Factors to consider

It is increasingly being felt worldwide that language should be taught in a manner consistent with local cultural expectations (McKay 2004). By the same token, it is argued that teacher development courses need to facilitate English teachers to develop their pedagogic competence within the context of local and cultural settings. Bangladesh, like many other developing countries, operates within its own specific set of circumstances and therefore the concern has been to look for principles that can form the basis for a culture-friendly approach to teacher development. The argument that is being forwarded in this paper has the following features as its reference points: teachers's belief systems, teachers's cultural orientations, and the contextual features within the country.

Belief systems

Cognition studies have established that beliefs and attitudes influence all human perception and the ways in which events are understood and acted upon. In other words, meaning is culturally embedded and socially constructed. Pajares (1992) claims that belief systems are an important construct in education, and they play a critical role in shaping teachers' perception and behaviour. Therefore, by the time prospective teachers enter a training college, their beliefs are well formed and are resistant to change. These beliefs are seen as complex and difficult to unpack, and what is more, they act as a 'unique filter' (Johnson 1992, 440). In other words, belief systems have a filtering effect on thinking and information processing.

Based on this assumption, it is important that teacher education and teacher educators appreciate the phenomenon of teacher beliefs. Most studies on teacher preparation programmes attest to the fact that teacher beliefs about their roles and about teaching remain largely unchanged during training. If we accept the above statement unconditionally, we may be confronted with the question 'Why then bother to train teachers?' The answer fortunately lies in additional insights from cognitive psychology.

These insights speak of multiple 'knowledges' constructed rather than stored, and learning which involves continuous active 'construction', 'connection' and 'reconstruction' of experiences within personalised contexts. Guba and Lincoln (1994) claim that these multiple constructions are subject to 'continuous revision' with 'changes likely to occur' when relatively different constructions are brought into juxtaposition in a 'dialectical context'. These 'different constructions' may be perceived as the 'received wisdom' or conventional knowledge imparted in teacher development courses, and the 'dialectical context' falls within the purview of the interaction of multiple views within the course. This cognitive approach supports the need for programmes to provide opportunities for trainee teachers to understand the dynamics of how they think and act as they learn to teach by engaging in such activities that enable them to make sense of what they are being presented.

Cultural orientations and contextual features

The word 'culture', in its traditional sense, is seen as the social milieu that provides a group with a shared construction of reality, a tradition and a recipe for action (Berry et al. 1992). The rules of culture are transmitted through a learning process, either tacit or conscious. We are thus faced with educational culture, classroom culture, examination culture, and teaching and learning styles embodied in our culture and woven into the context and the environment.

Moreover, contextual features such as resource availability and/or constraints, logistics and infrastructure are significant to the educational phenomenon in any setting. At the same time, as pointed out by Cortazzi and Jin (1996), there are clearly centralising tendencies of national syllabuses and examinations and widely used textbooks and notebooks, as well as clear perceptions of a common practice among teachers within a local context.

Byram and Fleming (1998), among others, advocate that educational developers need to orientate themselves with the macro aspects of the culture and the exigencies of the wider educational context in order to enable them to perceive the varied elements in the user culture and most importantly, to consider them as factors to be taken into account rather than as constraints to be overcome.

An example can be drawn from the element of routinisation that is highly favoured by the traditional work culture of Bangladesh. It is seen that teacher instructional behaviour in classrooms is understood as 'routines' (Prabhu 1992) which provide relative security and stability for teachers. Rahman's (2003) study of teachers' perceptions and attitudes towards the communicative form of teaching–learning also points to the presence of a set of ingrained beliefs and behavioural patterns in college teachers, tantamount to routinised behaviour. Although the idea of routinised behaviour goes against the notion of autonomy and creativity proposed by current progressive approaches to teacher education, the element of routinisation in the Bangladeshi teaching culture may be turned to advantage and converted into a positive factor rather than being treated as a constraint.

In order to explain the above claim, I turn to the area of rural development. Mascarenhas (1993) has attributed success in South Asian rural development to the importance of routine—good practices are routinised, and they lead to positive results. If we extend this statement to teacher education, we may argue that teacher training needs to be presented in such a manner that ideas may be incorporated as routines. Let us take the notion of reflection by teachers.

Current teacher education literature (Wallace 1996, Richards and Lockhart 1996, Richards 1998, Bailey 2003) has singled out reflection as a prominent activity that enables trainees to reconstruct their pedagogical values about teaching and learning in a manner that they find meaningful. If this element of reflection can be treated under the umbrella of routinisation, it may be used to advantage, or the element of reflection, analysis and interpretation may be used with such regularity that this practice becomes routinised in the trainee's repertoire.

These three factors, the cognitive, the cultural and the contextual, taken together provide a rationale for promoting a multi-layered orientation to ESL teacher development. Significantly then, in any teacher education/development undertaking (initial, in-service, short/long), teacher educators need to recognise and incorporate these issues. They need to aim at a process through which trainee teachers are able 'to make sense of', or understand and engage with, what is being proposed. The programme needs to relate to their mental constructs, their knowledge and their reasoning and needs to work within the social and contextual realities of their environment and their very existence.

Additional factors

Three additional factors need to be considered within the specific setting of Bangladesh. These are as follows.

a. The necessity of an *English language improvement component* in a teacher development course. Without an acceptable level of English competence, teachers cannot be expected to perform effectively in class despite the training they receive. Often teachers 'mis-teach' rather than teach. Indeed, English pronunciation problems and 'Banglish' structures are largely the result of a never-ending vicious circle of 'mis-teaching' by teachers with poor proficiency in English.
b. The need for the *training of simple atomistic skills of teaching and classroom management*, including the effective use of the blackboard and the efficient use of time. Our teachers often do not have these basic skills which disadvantage them in the classroom.
c. Moreover, the programme as such needs to recognise the need for teacher education to offer *methodologies particular to subject areas.* In terms of this, methodologies specific to English language becomes a priority. Importantly then, teacher educators need to be subject specialists too.

A teacher development study

Morris (2004) presents a study analysing a teacher development programme in Bangladesh which works within the framework of working with teacher beliefs and the local culture. The reflective approach to changing attitudes and mindsets was exemplified in a

2-week intensive training programme of seventeen teacher educators from the different TTCs in Bangladesh. They were taken through a self-directed strategy of reviewing the current BEd English elective course by hands-on re-planning of the twenty-two weeks of the course (three classes of ninety minutes each every week), including introductions in week 1 and evaluations in week 23. Through a series of directed study, assessment procedures and capacity building exercises, the teacher educators made revisions in the content as well as in the methodology of the BEd course. The report on the training programme claims that the teacher educators' evaluation was productive and encouraging. The dynamism they displayed was impressive and 'gives cause for optimism about the ability of the teacher educators to pursue their own CPD (Continuing Professional Development) sustainably and enthusiastically in future' (Morris 2004). This appears to tie in with Ramani (1987, 5), who has argued that 'teachers' theoretical abilities can be engaged and strengthened if their intuitions are accorded value and if the entry point is close to their experience as practising teachers'.

A caveat, however. This was a 2-week training programme especially arranged with an expatriate trainer. The Bangladeshi teacher educators were removed from their normal place of duty and placed with colleagues from other TTCs in a congenial environment, undertaking activities within a set target of time, place and resources where they functioned very well. Whether their 'enthusiasm and dynamism' would be carried back to their own work places and whether their attempts at motivating other colleagues would find equal response remains a question. Educational innovation literature is replete with stories of exasperation and failure when newly trained teacher educators try to bring fresh ideas to their colleagues. Therefore, this project needs follow-up assessment over a sufficient length of time.

Concluding remarks

It is widely accepted that adequate ESL teacher education is a powerful instrument for addressing the wide-ranging maladies afflicting the teaching of English in the curriculum. Having developed my argument from cognitive, cultural and contextual perspectives, I have emphasised their importance in understanding the phenomenon of teachers' construction of knowledge, their interpretation of the world around them and their orientation towards teaching. Within the teacher development course design, I have emphasised the centrality of trainee teachers' beliefs and an interaction with these beliefs in order to enable them to make sense of the training process.

Other assumptions that go beyond the training programme are that

a. teachers are more likely to change their attitudes and skills by working in their classrooms and schools and by working closely with other teachers;
b. this change can only happen with the full understanding and support of head teachers, local education officials and other stakeholders; and
c. belonging to forums and platforms enable interchange of ideas and develop confidence. Thus, teachers associations, teachers newsletters, participation in seminars, workshops, networking in cluster groups, action research, all need to be encouraged.

It is further suggested that just as I have argued for educators to accept and work with trainee perspectives and characteristics, so too should trainee teachers on entering the classroom, be able to extend similar loyalties to their students and *their* characteristics. This would allow teachers to dispel deep-rooted prejudices about learners. Such a conceptual shift can only be seen as empowering the ESL teacher with a renewed sense of professional responsibility.

Finally, it needs to be recognised that new approaches introduced solely into teacher education curriculum and training are unlikely to be sustained if they are not underpinned by parallel developments in English teaching pedagogy within the whole school system. Reforms need to be woven into teacher education programmes in a meaningful way and be sustained through a supportive infrastructure over the long term—a long-range investment in a total system rather than a one-off arrangement. The ESL teacher training provision system needs to take into account all the elements of a total instructional package. Indeed, significant professional change is a long, ongoing and cooperative process. It cannot happen in a single training course.

References

Bailey, K.M. 2003. Language Teaching Journals and Reflective Teaching. In *IATEFL 2003 Brighton Conference Selections,* ed. A. Pulverness. Kent: IATEFL.

Berry, J.W., et al. 1992. *Cross-cultural Psychology: Research and Implications.* Cambridge: Cambridge University Press.

Byram, M & M. Fleming, eds. 1998. *Language Learning in Intercultural Perspectives*. Cambridge: Cambridge University Press.

Cortazzi, M. and L. Jin. 1996. Cultures of Learning: Language Classrooms in China". In *Society and the Language Classroom,* ed. H. Coleman. Cambridge: Cambridge University Press.

Guba, E.G. and Y.S. Lincoln. 1994. Competing Paradigms in Qualitative Research. In *Handbook of Qualitative Research*, eds. N.K. Denzin and Y.S. Lincoln. Thousand Oaks, CA: Sage Publications.

Johnson, K.E. 1992. Learning to Teach: Instructional Actions and Decisions of Pre-service ESL Teachers. *TESOL Quarterly* Vol 26/3: 507533.

Kachru, B.B. 1996. South Asian English: Towards an Identity in Diaspora. In *South Asian English. Structure, Use and Users,* ed. R. J. Baumgardner. Illinois: University of Illinois Press.

Khan, R.S. and C. Taylor. 1993. *A Feasibility Study Consultancy for English Language Centres in Bangladesh*. Dhaka: The British Council.

Khan. R. 2003. Impact Assessment of an In-service Teacher Training Programme in Bangladesh. *NELTA Journal* Vol. 7, No. 1, 2: 34–47.

Markee, N. 1997. *Managing Curricular Innovation.* Cambridge: Cambridge University Press.

Mascarenhas, R.C. 1993. Explaining Success in South Asian Rural Development: The Importance of Routine. *Public Administration and Development* Vol 13: 457–487.

McKay, S.L. 2004. Teaching English as an International Language: The Role of Culture in Asian Contexts. *The Journal of Asia TEFL* Vol 1, No. 1. Spring 2004: 1–22.

Morris, A. 2004. BEd Curriculum for English Language Teaching: Report on Bangladesh. In *PROMOTE English Language Consultancy Report*. Dhaka: PROMOTE.

Nwagwu, C.C. 1997. The Environment of Crises in the Nigerian Education System. *Comparative Education* Vol 33/1: 87–95.

Pajares, M.F. 1992. Teachers' Beliefs and Educational Research Cleaning Up a Messy Construct. *Review of Educational Research*. Vol 62: 307–322.

Prabhu, N.S. 1992. The Dynamics of the Language Lesson. *TESOL Quarterly* Vol 26/2: 225–241.

PROMOTE. 2004. *Final report: 6th year External Review Mission, May-June 2004*. 24 June 2004 Dhaka: PROMOTE.

Ramani, E. 1987. Theorizing from the Classroom. *English Language Teaching Journal* Vol 41/1: 3–11.

Rahman, A. 1988. English Language Teaching in Bangladesh: Problems and Prospects. *Journal of the Institute of Modern Languages* Vol 3: 94–111.

________. 2003. Forthcoming. College Teachers' Perceptions of ELT: Relevance to Teacher Training. In *English Language Teaching in South Asia*, ed. S. Mansoor. Pakistan: Oxford University Press.

Richards, J. C. 1998. *Beyond Training*. Cambridge: Cambridge University Press.

Richards, J. C. and C. Lockhart. 1996. *Reflective Teaching in Second Language Classrooms.* Cambridge: Cambridge University Press.

Wallace, M. 1996. Structured Reflection: The Role of the Professional Project in Training ESL Teachers. In *Teacher Learning in Language Teaching*, eds. D. Freeman and J. C. Richards Cambridge: Cambridge University Press.

Contributors

Rama Kant Agnihotri
Professor, Department of Linguistics, Delhi University

E. Annamalai
Visiting Professor, Yale Center for International and Area Studies, Yale University

Robert Bellarmine
Director, 3E: English for Empowerment & Enrichment, Chennai

George Stanley Braine
Professor, Department of English, The Chinese University of Hong Kong

K. Chellappan
formerly, Director, State Institute of English, Chennai

Probal Dasgupta
Professor, Linguistic Research Unit, Indian Statistical Institute, Kolkata

Premakumari Dheram
Professor, Centre for Materials Development, English and Foreign Languages University (formerly, CIEFL) Hyderabad

Greta Gorsuch
Associate Professor, Department of Classical and Modern Languages and Literatures, Texas Tech University, Texas

Dale Thomas Griffee
Professor, Department of English, Texas Tech University, Texas

Thiru Kandiah
formerly, Professor, Department of English, University of Peradeniya, Sri Lanka; presently, Honorary Adjunct Professor, Department of Languages and Intercultural Education, Curtin University of Technology, Australia

Lachman M. Khubchandani
Professor, Centre for Communication Studies, Pune

Sabiha Mansoor
Professor, Centre of English Language, Aga Khan University, Pakistan

Marie Perera
Head, Department of Humanities Education, University of Colombo, Sri Lanka

V. Prakasam
Professor, School of Distance Education, English and Foreign Languages University (formerly, CIEFL), Hyderabad

Arifa Rahman
Professor, Department of English, Presidency University, Bangladesh

Jacob Tharu
formerly, Professor of Evaluation, CIEFL, Hyderabad

Stefano Vassere
Archivio di Stato del Cantone Ticino, Bellinzona, Switzerland

Index

About the Author

Imtiaz Anees is an equestrian Olympian, trainer, competitor, NBC commentator, qualified Level 2 instructor and coach educator.

Born in India, studied in Australia and based in the United States, Imtiaz has had the opportunity to work with three-day eventing, dressage, showjumping and racehorses. Having travelled nearly half the globe, he has been fortunate to have worked and trained with some of the best riders in Australia, England, France, New Zealand, Switzerland and the United States. Internationally, he has competed at the Sydney Olympics in 2000 and the World Equestrian Games in Spain in 2002. 'Imti', as he is lovingly called by all in the equine world, has won a bronze medal at the Asian Games in Thailand and a bronze medal at the Asia Pacific Games in Australia. He has managed the showjumping stables of His Highness Sayyid Shabib Bin Taimur of Oman and worked at the Nanoli stud farm, owned by one of the biggest names in the horse world, Khushroo Dhunjibhoy.

He has, to his credit, successfully conceptualized and executed several events in equestrian, and some of his students are competing internationally today. In his last role, Imtiaz was the head of department of the equestrian programme at the New England Girls High School in Australia. He holds a degree in horse management from Marcus Oldham College, Australia, and has completed an equitation course at the Ecole Nationale d' Equitation Saumur, France.

As the only equestrian Olympian in India, he wants to share his knowledge and experience with all other riders and offers internship programmes to teach equine management. He runs an equestrian training centre—Seahorse Equestrian, a boutique stable with sixteen horses. It's, on a beautiful beach in a small fishing village in Nargol, Gujarat. His key objective is to bring professionalism to the sport in India and equip riders to work and ride internationally.

He lives by his personal motto: Discipline, Determination, and Dedication.

You can connect with Imtiaz at:

www.imtiazanees.com

imtiazanees@hotmail.com